Before I ever knew how to pray or to whom to pray, I begged for escape from my agony. I wanted, and plotted, simply for a way out. Yet, God in His mercy knew the plans He had for my life.

ଓ

"Now all glory to God, who is able, through his mighty power at work within us, to accomplish infinitely more than we might ask or think."
(EPHESIANS 3:20; NLT)

D1044264

Sт. Ретегsбцгд, Яцssга, Иоцембег 1997

Even in the summer months the average temperature in St. Petersburg rarely rises to 70° and in the winters it can be brutally cold. It had been some time since I had had a meal and even longer since I had had a job. Not knowing what to expect, I knocked hopefully at the door of Mark and Melinda Cathey, American missionaries in Russia.

Melinda answered the door. Hoping she would remember me from when we had met briefly a year earlier, I was disappointed when it became clear she did not know who I was. "What can I do for you?" she asked.

I admitted that I was looking for work, and I offered to cook for them.

"Sorry," Melinda responded. "We don't need a cook."

Mark joined us and the three of us had a nice polite conversation, but I left dejected and discouraged. Before I left I gave them my phone number and uttered a final plea. "I can also be a tour guide, or clean your house, or baby-sit, or be a translator ..."

A few days later I was pleased when the Catheys followed up and invited me to their home for dinner. Apparently they had not been able to get their Russian visitor off of their minds.

When I arrived, Melinda asked, "Where's your coat, Alex?" I explained to her that I had given it to an orphan.

Over dinner Mark asked, "When was the last time you had meat?" I admitted to him that I couldn't remember. My diet was pretty much just cheap starchy foods like potatoes and noodles.

As we ate I shared with them some of my life story and talked about the work I was doing with Russian orphanages. Looking back, it is obvious that the Lord had planned this encounter. Little did we know that the friendship that began when two American missionaries opened their door to a nineteen-year-old hungry Russian stranger would end up impacting the lives of countless orphans in the former Soviet Union and lead to the starting of a ministry that would change all of our lives.

1

*"Before I formed you in the womb I knew you, and
before you were born I consecrated you ..."*
—*Jeremiah 1:5*

St. Petersburg is on the Baltic Sea near the border of
Russia and Finland. One of the most beautiful cities
in the world, it is named for Peter the Great, the Russian
Tsar who founded the city in 1703 and spared no expense
in making it the showplace of his empire. For two cen-
turies it was the spiritual and political capital of Russia.
When the Communists came to power they changed the
name to Leningrad and moved the capital to Moscow.

Because it is so far north there are only a few hours of
daylight during the winter. On one of those winter days—
December 6, 1977—a woman came to one of the state hos-
pitals in Leningrad, no doubt afraid and almost certainly
alone, and gave birth to a healthy baby boy with dark hair
and brown eyes. That baby was me. I know from medical
records that I weighed seven pounds and was twenty-two
inches long. The records also indicate that for the first
three days I was with my mother in the hospital. She was
young, only eighteen or nineteen.

God only knows the weight of the decisions she pon-
dered those three days as she held her newborn baby. And
only God knows if her decision was selfish or selfless; if she
was thinking of herself, or thinking of my best interests.

What we do know is that when she left the hospital she promptly discarded me in the closest dumpster.

I have often felt God's hand of mercy and blessing on me. Surely the first time it was evident was later that day when someone heard me crying and retrieved me from the trash heap. They returned me to the hospital, thanks to the identification tag still on my tiny wrist. The police and appropriate social agencies were notified but when they finally tracked down my mother, she refused to come for me. She was young and said she had no means to care for me. Her decision that cold and dark December day set the direction for my life.

She signed over all parental rights, and I became a ward of the Soviet State. I was sent to a "nourishment house" for infants, the first of several Russian orphanages that would become my homes.

It was in this "house," Orphanage Number 9, that I would live until April 1982 when, at the age of four, I was transferred to Orphanage Number 6. (Though the Russians have written some of the greatest works of literature and music, our creativity apparently does not extend to naming orphanages.) I have no memories of my first orphanage or my caretakers and surroundings, but I do have my medical records—the only tangible evidence of my early years.

Written on what Americans would call theme book paper, I have carried them with me wherever I have gone. Now a little yellowed and worn, they represent the sum total of what I know about my early life. When I show them to people they are surprised to see, tucked amongst the pages of the medical booklet, a birth certificate. Even though it is in Russian, it is obvious that in addition to my own name it lists names for both a father and mother. I have to quickly point out that this particular birth certificate is marked a "duplicate." Over the years, every time I was moved to a new orphanage I was given my records to take with me, and each time I received a new birth certificate and the parents' names were different. I do not put much stock in the validity of those names, so I do not know who my parents were, or are, or anything about them.

Sadly, all of my other records have been lost.

Regardless of the inaccuracies of the document, it does provide official documentation of my birth: Alexander Victorovich Krutov, December 6, 1977. Since Russian children always bear our fathers' names as our own middle names it is conceivable that my father's name was Victor.

Reading through the medical records it is safe to say that they really tell the story of those early years. It seems that for my first four years I was in the hospital more than I was at the orphanage. I was first hospitalized when I was one month old. Noted in the records, I was treated for "psycho-neurological problems and second level maldystrophy (malnutrition)." I had chicken pox and pneumonia in both lungs in 1978 when I was only one year old.

The information found in my medical records marks milestones of my early life, in some ways the next best thing to a mother keeping a baby book. At ten months I was able to hold my head up on my own and able to roll over. At fifteen months I first began walking while holding on to things. I was twenty-one months before I was walking on my own. At fourteen months I got my first teeth and one month after my second birthday I spoke my first words. The records note that at twenty months I was independently dressing myself and that at three years I had fully-developed speech. There were several instances of major colds or flu with high fevers and hospitalizations.

Perhaps the saddest of the maladies is the note that in 1978, when less than a year old, I was treated for an "abscess on his buttocks." Years later as I have visited orphanages the probable cause has become obvious: for the most part, in the crowded and understaffed Russian orphanages babies just lie in their cribs, all day, every day. As a baby I had bed sores on my bottom from lying in a crib with no one to pick me up or rock me to sleep.

It is not uncommon for adopted Russian orphans, no matter how loved and cuddled they may be by their new families, to still rock themselves back and forth in order to fall asleep. With no one to hold you and rock you to sleep, you learn how to do it yourself. It breaks my heart to think how many more little ones are still over there in orphanages where cribs line the walls, side by side, babies rocking themselves to sleep at night and suffering bed sores from laying in their cribs all day.

2

He heals the brokenhearted and binds their wounds.

—Psalm 147:3

When I was four I was moved to Orphanage Number 6 in St. Petersburg; it is from there my earliest memories stem. I was only at this orphanage for a couple of years, and most of my memories there are good ones. We had food and clothing and caretakers to tend to us, doctors to care for us in sickness. Cooks prepared daily meals for us that kept us from going hungry. All the needs that we were aware of at that young age were met.

Orphanage Number 6 is where I met Edik (or Edward), whose parents had abandoned him. We became best friends. That's also where I met Misha. The three of us remain lifelong friends. Unlike my earliest years, I rarely got sick once I got to Orphanage 6. My medical records show that I was hospitalized only once during that time.

While I have rather fond memories of the place, the first thing that actually springs to mind when I think back on Orphanage 6 is the rats. We had lots of rats and we were all afraid of them. Misha, Ed, and I would often see them in the window-well of the dining room window.

And sadly this was also the place where I first experienced the death of one of my fellow orphans. One of the caretakers locked a little boy in the basement for punishment and forgot that he was there. He died, all alone, locked in that basement room. When they eventually found him, the rats had been feeding on his body for days.

There were two hundred to three hundred orphans in Orphanage Number 6, which made it one of the smaller orphanages in Russia. Each summer we would be taken for three months to a *dacha*, as country homes are known in Russia. It was about two hours outside St. Petersburg and we stayed in cabins around the property.

While most of my recollections of the *dacha* are pleasant there is one horrific memory that stands out. This was the first time that we experienced a murder. The cabins had no running water, so we had to use outhouses. Most of us younger boys were afraid to go out at night so they set an aluminum bucket in the middle of the room for us to use at night if we didn't want to go to the outhouse. One of my classmates decided to demonstrate his bravery and ventured out in the night to use the outhouse. He was found the next morning, stabbed to death. A prisoner, who had escaped from a nearby prison, was later caught and charged with the murder.

I have been asked what kind of comfort we received from the caretakers after this traumatic event. My answer is a quick one: None. The whole thing was treated very matter-of-factly. We did head back to the orphanage earlier than planned. I remember how special we all felt to have our twenty or so buses escorted by police as we made our way back through the city and back "home" to Orphanage 6.

There was no formal school or classroom in the orphanage. I do remember a time in our living room when they were trying to teach all of us kids our colors, shapes, and alphabet—an informal preschool of sorts. But most of this did not sink in for any of us. When we later went on to formal school, none of us knew our alphabet or colors or shapes.

Even at this young age there was no room for individuality. We were always treated as a big group. We all dressed similarly. When we went on any outings it was obvious that we were a group of orphans and it just fed the stigma that we were "nobodies." The Soviet Union was socialist so the State provided for our needs, along with everyone else's. We had new clothes, not hand-me-downs. But in true Soviet style, all of our clothes were the same and we received them just once a year: three sets of each article of clothing, including underwear. While we each might receive three new sweaters, they would be the same three sweaters everyone else got. "New Clothes Day" was the best day of the year since it was the only day I had something brand new that belonged only to me. But that would only last a few days because before long everyone's shirts and pants and socks and underwear would get mixed up.

Misha, Ed, and I all cried when we were told we were being moved to Orphanage Number 51. We were frightened by the unknown. We were leaving the only place we had known as home. Our only consolation was that we were moving on together.

3

For I am the Lord, your God, who takes hold of your right hand and says to you, Do not fear; I will help you.

—Isaiah 41:13

Orphanage Number 51 was enormous. It housed between five hundred and six hundred orphans. On the first floor was the dining room, which was huge. But I soon found out that it still wasn't big enough to hold all of the kids that lived there. At meal time we all had to hold hands and file down quietly to line up for dinner. It usually took four shifts to get us all through a meal and we had to stand quietly in the line, waiting our turn to go in and sit down and eat.

I remember arriving at Orphanage 51 the first day. As we stood in the foyer I was awed at how big it was. I was staring up at the huge chandelier, amazed at the size of this thing, when suddenly one of the huge glass globes came crashing down and shattered in pieces right in front of me. Looking back now, that was probably pretty symbolic of what was going to happen to my life in Orphanage 51.

For the first time Misha, Ed, and I were in with boys up to the age of seventeen. From day one the older boys were extremely frightening to us—a fear that was well-founded. They incessantly bullied all of us younger boys. They were notorious for forcing the young boys to drink and smoke and swear. If a boy refused, the older ones would beat him until he did. Ed and I refused. We were labeled "the Aristocrats" because the older boys felt like we thought we were too good for the rest of them. More than anyone else, Ed and I were beaten by the bullies.

All of us boys lived on the fourth floor, thirty or forty to a bedroom. The beds were so close you had to turn sideways to walk between them and there was no other furniture in the bedrooms.

We had free time every day from about 3:00 to 5:00 after school. While we were not supposed to leave the grounds, we all did. There was a bread factory right next door. Despite the concrete wall and the barbed wire fencing, kids would sneak into the factory and steal bread. They often gave it to the older boys to bribe them into not beating them.

While the government did not allow charity and deemed it unlawful to give handouts (the State, after all, took care of its own) a lot of the kids used their free time to beg for handouts. Occasionally they would get enough in handouts to go down the street and buy themselves ice cream. I never begged or stole, but I did use my free time to wander the streets, keeping my head down in hopes that I would find money people had dropped. Sometimes I found enough to reward myself with ice cream. Orphans could also go to the movie house for free (state-provided, of course) so I spent many afternoons watching movies, a seven-year-old, alone in the movie theater.

Orphanage 51 was attached to a Soviet boarding school for linguistics, specializing in teaching English. It was rather an elite school and the children attending the boarding school were not orphans. Their parents chose to send them there for their education. It would have been a great educational opportunity for us but six months after

I arrived the State shut down the boarding school. However, it did allow our already overcrowded orphanage to expand into the old school building. Fortunately for me, Ed, Misha, and all of our first grade classmates, we were able to escape to the "new" building. All fifty or sixty of our age group were moved into four rooms in the attached school building.

The building was actually an old palace and the rooms were large and beautiful. There were gorgeous marble fireplaces, ornate light fixtures, big mirrors, and fancy woodwork. We first graders had two rooms for bedrooms, one for a playroom, and one for a classroom, as well as our very own bathroom. I remember lots of locked doors throughout the place so that we could not roam. But even with parts of the building closed off to us we were thrilled to have a space of our own. We called it our "great escape." While we still had to interact with the older bullies and other boys all during the day, at least at night we felt safe in our own space.

Nighttime was our time. All of the caregivers who worked there during the day left to go home around nine. There was only one night caretaker for the entire floor— about two hundred kids. Orphans or not, kids will be kids, and nighttime became our best playtime. We would take the covers off our beds and pull each other, slipping and sliding, all over the parquet floors. If we got caught I was always the one who got punished because I was always giggling the loudest. The caretaker hated all of us, but hated me most and thought I was a troublemaker. She took every chance she got to make me an example for the others.

We would hear her coming and rush back to our beds and throw ourselves under the covers. She would storm into the room and even though all forty of us were giggling under the covers she would head straight for my bed, rip off the covers, and beat me in the face with her shoe.

Early in my years at Orphanage 51 I had to be taken to the hospital for some kind of treatment for one of my eyes; I don't remember what, exactly. One of the few male caretakers offered to escort me to the hospital. It promised to be a great adventure—my first "official" time out of the orphanage and into the city. Riding the Metro was certainly a new and thrilling experience.

On the way home from the hospital, the caretaker took me to his apartment to show me around. He then proceeded to beat me and attempted to molest me. I kicked, screamed, and pushed. He could have used force and as a little boy I could not have defended myself. Fortunately, though, my protests were enough for him and he gave up. He grabbed me by the arm and roughly escorted me back to the orphanage. As soon as I could I reported the incident to the orphanage director. I never saw the man working at the orphanage again (today they rarely allow male caregivers in the orphanages in Russia because of all the problems they had with molestation and abuse).

There were no showers in Orphanage 51 and no hot water. We would "bathe" each day by splashing ourselves with cold water at the sink. For six days we would wear the same clothes, including underwear. Once a week we got to wash our clothes. There was a large wooden bench in the bathroom where we would spread our clothes out and then rub them down with a big old bar of soap. Then we would take them to the sink and rinse them out in cold water. We strung rope from the pipes in the bathroom and hung our clothes to dry. You were never assured you were actually getting your own clothes back, and never assured that whatever clothes you did get would be dry or clean! Ed and I would often sneak into the bathroom to wash our socks and underwear throughout the week. None of the other kids cared, but they stunk so bad and the two of us couldn't stand it.

Once a week we were taken to the public bathhouse. That was always a frightening experience for the young boys. We had soap but no shampoo and we didn't get showers—just a bucket of hot water with which to bathe. (This might explain why I enjoy taking incredibly long hot showers today!)

In my early years at Orphanage 51 I became sickly again. I had repeated bouts of pneumonia, a hernia, and chronic stomach problems. Four years in a row I was in the hospital for a month each year, with doctors trying to diagnose my stomach ailment. My medical records simply indicate "chronic gastroenteritis/ulcer" repeatedly. I was in almost constant pain for years and I lost a lot of weight. I was sick or hospitalized so much that I had to repeat the first grade because I had missed so much of the school year.

As I think back on my early years in the orphanage system, one of the things that strikes me again and again is the lack of individuality. We were dressed the same, fed the same, treated the same, and had the same schedule. Every morning we were gathered all together, lined up in the foyer, and made to recite stuff. We received pins as we progressed up the different levels of the Communist Party. I remember receiving a red star with a picture of Lenin on it. It was all so "Soviet"! It was easy to feel like a nobody. I was not an individual, just one of thousands upon thousands of Russian orphans. There was no room for privacy or dignity. And there was absolutely no individualized attention or affection.

Yet looking back over those years I can tell that God was marking me for His own, long before I knew Him. To the caretakers I was known as "the troublemaker." To the bullies I was known as one of "the Aristocrats." Whether it was out of pride, stubbornness, or God's hand of protection on me, I don't know, but I refused to be bullied into drinking or smoking or swearing. I never followed the crowd over the barbed wire fence to steal bread. I refused to beg for money or food, and chose, rather, to wander the streets alone. And God was about to affirm His calling on my life with a very special blessing.

4

*I lift up my eyes to the hills—where does my help
   come from?
My help comes from the Lord, the Maker of heaven
   and earth.*

Psalm 121:1–2

During my first year at Orphanage 51 I had many different caretakers, but just one teacher, Irina. She was our teacher from first grade all the way through fifth. She had taught at the boarding school until it closed; when she taught our first grade class it was her first year teaching at the orphanage.

Irina made it very clear to us what her role was to be. "I am not your mother," she warned us. "I am your teacher. Do not hug me. Do not kiss me. Do not slobber on me, and do not *ever* call me 'Momma.' I am here because I am being paid to teach you."

Not surprisingly, she was a very strict teacher and she scared all of us. She was a stickler about our posture and insisted we sit up straight in our chairs at all times. She would smack us with her pointer if she caught us slouching. She would also smack our hands if she caught us talking in class.

Irina would take us on field trips to the "Houses of Culture," education centers around St. Petersburg. They were open and free to the public. There were some for dance, some for photography, some for sports, and even some for sewing. Because the orphanage had minimal education supplies these should have been great opportunities for us to learn. If we had really understood the opportunity back then—if someone had really motivated us to learn—we might have appreciated them. But all we could think was, Why do we need or want to learn photography when we will never use it? We would rather use our free time hunting for money for ice cream.

In September of 1986, just before I turned nine, a woman named Melana Kozeeva became caretaker for twenty-six of us boys and girls at Orphanage 51. To this day I remember the first time I met her. She was the most beautiful woman I had ever seen. You could feel the love she had in her heart. She told us, "You may call me 'Momma' if you like, as long as no other adults are around. I will love you and care for you and I promise you this: I will protect you from harm." Those were easily the most comforting words I had ever heard in my whole life.

Looking back on that day, Melana says, "My heart was washed with a warm wave of joy and thanks to God for this opportunity to work with all these dear children." She says she remembered me as a tall, skinny child with curly dark hair. "You seemed so alive," she recalled. "As I got to know you, I realized there was no balance to your emotions. If you were happy then everyone knew it from your hyperactivity, joyful screams, and contagious laughter. Yet from time to time you were very angry or very sad and your responses were as pronounced as when you were happy. You clearly needed strong leadership and I felt you needed a person whom you could trust."

At 7:30 each morning Melana would wake us up and help us get ready for the day. She would then take us down

As is common with orphans, pictures of my childhood are scarce amd the quality is poor. This was taken at the sanatorium. That's me on the right in the light shirt. Also in the picture are Melana (seated in the center). Maria is sitting next to her. Edik is the little boy with the dark hair on the left

to breakfast and walk us to our classroom. We were in class every day from 9:00 to about 2:30, at which time Melana would come back for us.

The big kids still bullied us, of course. With so many kids to watch over, Melana couldn't be everywhere at once, but if she did catch the bullies picking on one of her boys she chased after them waving a broomstick. The older boys soon learned not to mess with her.

In the orphanage only ten to fifteen percent of us were "true" orphans—those who had been abandoned by our parents and signed over to the State. The rest were known as "social orphans." They had at least one parent but they were taken away from their parents by the State because of abuse, alcoholism, or crime, and placed in the orphanage system. Because these parents never had their parental rights terminated, that meant almost all of my classmates would go home for weekends and holidays. Initially, that made those of us who remained sad. But we soon realized what an advantage we had: Melana began taking turns taking us home with her on weekends.

My friend Misha was a social orphan and often went home on weekends, but Edik and I spent many a weekend with Melana and her family. Ed and I got to know her daughters and sons-in-law, her husband, and even her parents (we always called them *dedulya* and *babulya*, Russian for grandpa and grandma). They lived about thirty miles outside of town in a *dacha*. While they had electricity they did not have any running water or heat. As a result, their *dacha* was where I learned to do physical work.

I had never seen a well before but I soon learned to draw water from theirs, as well as to cut firewood to heat the house. Melana's family made Ed and me feel welcome and told us they wanted us to come as often as possible, but, of course, Melana had to take turns with all of the kids.

Melana loved all of us and didn't show favoritism. We all knew, though, that she had a deeper love for Ed. He became like her son. She never legally adopted him, but we all knew. We didn't question that or resent it because she was so loving and protective of all of us. She was the closest thing to a mother I had ever known.

I did not consciously long for love or family; those were foreign words and concepts to me at that time. I had never experienced them. In the Soviet days adoption was very rare: there were no foreign adoptions, and not many Russians were looking to adopt. Once in the orphanage system most of us "true orphans" remained in it until we turned seventeen or eighteen. While I may not have realized my basic emotional needs, I knew, when Melana came into my life, that I was experiencing feelings I had never had. For the first time I felt loved and protected.

Wanting to get us away from the orphanage and the bad influence of the older boys, Melana managed to give us the most wonderful year in our young lives. When we were nine, she convinced the State to pay for her to take our class to a sanatorium for a whole year. It was a cross between a medical facility and a spa, though not nearly as nice and luxurious as American spas. This was a state-owned campus of concrete buildings, set in a remote resort area about twenty-five miles north of St. Petersburg. It had more park-like yard area than we had ever seen. Melana and Irina both went with us for the year, as our caretakers and teachers. The two women rotated weeks, so one week Irina would be both caretaker and teacher, and the next week she would leave and Melana would take her place.

The women justified this experiment to the State by telling them it would improve our health. We had physical therapy sessions, massage therapy, and chamomile and eucalyptus baths. We had nurses on duty who took turns for twenty-four-hour shifts. We could walk to the beach and play in the sand. We could hike in the woods. Melana took us berry picking and taught us to make pies. Obviously, this was a glorious existence for a bunch of nine-year-olds, and the happiest time of my life. (The only one downside was nap time. They still made us take naps at age nine, and I hated nap time!)

At the sanatorium we had television for the first time. We watched soap operas sometimes, then out in the woods we raked the leaves and pine needles and made little houses for ourselves and we would enact the soap operas, making up our own story lines. We had never in our lives had that kind of imaginative play at the orphanage.

At night there was a cartoon, *"Spokoinoiy Nochi Maliyshiy"* ("Good Night, Children"). Like a soap opera, the story line continued from day to day. It was the first kids show we had ever seen. We loved it and would never miss a night.

I couldn't have known at the time, of course, but as wonderful as all of it was—the time with Melana and her family, and the year at the sanatorium—it was only the calm before the storm. The circumstances of my life were about to change, and change drastically. This wonderful year was only a respite that would usher in one of the worst years of my young life.

Our group at the first sanatorium. Melana is on the far left. The little girl next to her is Sveta; the second boy from her is Edik. That's me at the top of the photo with the tilted head and black hair

5

At least there is hope for a tree: If it is cut down, it will sprout again, and its new shoots will not fail.
—Job 14:7

Melana's name derives from the Russian word *mela*, which means soft, kind, gentle. And that she was. The weeks with Melana at the sanatorium were like night and day from the weeks with Irina. We counted down the days until Melana would return.

All of the kids called her "Momma" except for me. I loved her, but I was never raised with maternal names in my vocabulary and even at that young age the word seemed too powerful, too meaningful, to use as a pretend word. After all, she was not my real mother. Still, because I loved her, I called her other endearing names I reserved just for her, like "Musik," or "Mima."

There was a beer stand just off the grounds of the sanatorium. Vacationers and townspeople often cut through the park on the sanatorium grounds to get from the beach to the beer stand. One day as we kids played in the park area a couple, Kolya and Larisa Proturnov, walked through. They saw all of us, but singled out me and a girl in my class named Maria to talk to. They wanted to know who we all were and why we were there. After talking with us they immediately went into the building and spoke with Melana, expressing an interest in adopting the two of us!

Kolya, the husband, was in his late thirties and an engineer at the telephone company. Larisa, the wife, was in her mid-thirties and worked at the post office.

There were few adoptions back then. None of us kids even talked about it. We didn't truly understand what it meant. Melana was a bit taken aback by Kolya and Larisa's desire. She asked how long they had been married and how many children of their own they had. She learned they were childless. She was caught off guard to hear them request to adopt not just one, but two children, especially since Melana knew how different our personalities were.

Because Maria was ten years old, a year older than I was, they would need written permission from Maria to adopt her. With me, only nine, that would not be necessary. Melana explained to the couple that adopting kids who were nine and ten years old was not the same as adopting babies, that it might be a difficult process for us to adapt. Nonetheless, the couple started the paperwork and the adoption process began.

Over the next few months as the paperwork made its way through the Soviet bureaucracy, the couple was given permission to take Maria and me for weekend visits to their home, about five minutes from the sanatorium.

Everything went well on those weekend visits. Maria gave her written permission and, for my part, I was very excited about the opportunity. So, just before I turned ten, I was legally adopted by Kolya and Larisa. (At the last minute they changed their mind and chose not to adopt Maria; I never learned why.) I went right from the sanatorium—and the only "family" I had ever known—to my new home.

Because I wasn't ten yet they did not even have to go to court to make it official. The couple asked me if I would be willing to change my name. I did not want my first name to change—that was the only identity I had ever known—but I did agree to change my middle name. With the official adoption papers I became Alexander Nickolay Proturnov. They also changed my birth date. I would have to go to public school now and they did not feel I was ready for the fourth grade, so they made me a year younger and enrolled me in the third grade, telling me they had no choice.

Public school was just the beginning of many "firsts" for me. They lived in a large two-story building. It was divided up for four families so our home was only two rooms. One room served as the kitchen and dining room, and now, my bedroom. The other room was the living room. With its foldout sofa bed it doubled as my parents' room. They hung a piece of fabric over a rope to give them privacy but that did not keep me from being subjected to my first exposure to the intimacy of husband and wife. I wanted to run out of there, but there was no place to go, so I'd hold my fingers in my ears so as not to hear them.

The house had no running water. We carried water from a well and used an outhouse, as well as the *banya*, or public bathhouse. The fireplace was the only heat we had and for that we had to chop our own wood. We had electricity, but we had to buy tanks of gas that were used to cook our food. In many respects, the conditions were no better than the orphanage, and on top of that I now had chores to do, like helping cut the firewood and hauling the water from the well.

Another first was going to church. My parents were Russian Orthodox and they took me to church with them each week. I loved it. There was no religion of any kind—and certainly no church services—at the orphanage. Irina was a strong atheist, and so were most of the staff.

Melana, though a strong Orthodox, never talked about it to us kids.

The Proturnovs had me baptized in the church and I felt very honored. That ritual, even though I did not understand it, meant a lot to me. While the overall experience of church was positive, there was no sense of a relationship with God in any of this. I didn't even understand who God was.

My new family also offered me my first experience at grocery shopping. In the Soviet Union you didn't just go to a grocery store for all your supplies. You went to the dairy for the milk, the bakery for the bread, and the market for the fruits and vegetables. In 1988 there was a real shortage of food in our country and everyone had food stamps. People had to wait in line, sometimes as long as seven or eight hours, to buy two loaves of bread (all a family was allowed per week). I vividly remember standing in line for seven hours, only to have them run out of bread and turn away those of us still in line. People were really struggling in the Soviet Union at that time, but as orphans, we had been spared much of this, so this was eye-opening for me.

The adjustment to public school was made all the more difficult by two things. First, I was starting school in the middle of the school year. Second, my parents made the mistake of telling everyone that I was adopted. Adoption was so uncommon—so odd, in the eyes of the other children—that I became the victim of merciless teasing by my forty or so classmates. My teacher was an angry, mean woman in her late seventies who could neither see nor hear well. While I was able somehow to make a few friends, I was moved to the back of the class for talking.

We had some textbooks, but we mostly listened to the teacher. We kept *dnevnicks* (journals) in which we wrote

We shared this home with three other families.
Our two rooms were in the lower right corner

notes each day on all our subjects; at the end of the week, our journals would be turned in. Our grade would be based on the notes in our *dnevnick*, combined with our behavior in class.

From my very first journal, the teacher always failed me.

It seemed that no matter how hard I worked or how quiet I would try to be in class, I would receive a failing mark every time. While I was by no means a perfect student, I have to think that being labeled the orphan who talked in class helped the teacher write me off from the very start. She did not seem to have any intention of helping me learn, and she certainly did not intend to give me passing grades.

The first week I brought home my failing grade on my journal I presented it to my mother, ready to plead my case. She showed no concern or sympathy, and simply stated, "You'll have to talk with your dad when he gets home."

My father worked long hours at the phone company and usually didn't get home for dinner until after 7:00. I also had begun to notice that he smelled like alcohol most nights when he got home. Unfortunately, that night was no different. I took my journal to him and explained the situation as I saw it. He did not believe me. He made me strip off all of my clothes and proceeded to beat me with the big metal buckle of his leather belt. In his drunken rage he shouted out his expectations of his child. He wanted me to be a perfect son, an excellent student. "And," he added, "anything less than A's and B's and you'll get this beating again!"

My parents never visited the teacher and never tried to help me with my school work. True to his word, Dad continued to beat me every Friday when I brought my *dnevnick* home.

The failing grades and the beatings continued for about two months. At that time I decided that I had had enough of both and ran away—another first. The only place I knew to go was back to the sanatorium. As much as I wanted to run to the protection of Melana, I knew I couldn't. When Mom and Dad came there looking for me—which I was certain they would—Melana would have to tell the truth. Instead, I ran to my fellow orphans. They hid me in the closet, where I slept all night, hidden under clothes. During the day they would sneak me food.

This happened three or four times; each time my parents would call the police and the police would find me and take me back home. Melana wouldn't intervene because she thought I was just exaggerating and missed being with my friends. She thought I just needed time to adjust.

In true childlike fashion, it never occurred to me to run someplace else. I didn't know anyplace else. So imagine my shock the final time I ran to the sanatorium and found out my class had left and had gone back to Orphanage Number 51 in St. Petersburg. Now what was I going to do?

St. Petersburg was about twenty-five miles away. Surely my parents would not expect a ten-year-old boy to run away to the city. They would assume I was hiding somewhere near the sanatorium. So off to the city I went.

Over the next year I ran away over thirty times and headed for St. Petersburg each time, walking for hours and hours. Sometimes I would get picked up by the police before reaching the city. Many times I was picked up in the city, often being caught sleeping on a park bench (it took me a while to figure out that the park was right next to the police station!).

I got food scraps from garbage cans. Over time I learned to hide in the bushes when I saw a police officer. Often, I tried to find Orphanage Number 51. When I'd finally get there I would beg them to take me in. The director would always turn me away, shouting, "You are not an orphan! Go home!" slamming the door in my face.

Every single time I ran to the city the police would eventually find me and take me home. They never mistreated me or locked me in a cell. In fact, they were always very nice to me and I got on a first-name basis with most of them. The police would catch me, take me back to the station, give me food and tea, and just sit and talk with me while we waited for Valentina, the Inspector for Youth Rights.

Over time I got to know Valentina as well. We had good conversations and she usually gave me some money. At some point I started sneaking onto the train instead of walking into the city. I always thought I successfully fooled the conductor, but every time I got off the train in the city the police were right there waiting for me. By now I was eleven. I thought I was so clever, but in reality I was very naive. I was just a young boy, living alone on the streets, sometimes for weeks at a time, trying to evade my parents and the police, and never really succeeding.

This was my life for almost two years. I would go home and, in between the weekly beatings, life was pretty good. We would go to the movies. My parents would buy me new clothes. We would go to church. Then I would bring home my journal, get another beating, and run away again.

During this time my mother became pregnant and gave birth to a girl they named Maria. Not long after Maria was born my parents stopped sending the police to look for me. They didn't seem to care anymore. But by now, all the policemen knew me so the routine would continue, with a slight twist. They stopped taking me home; instead Valentina would just give me some money and tell me to go on home. Surprisingly, I did. I still don't understand why I kept going back home. Maybe I was just hoping that things would change.

The last time Valentina sent me on my way, she said, "Alex, the next time we won't put you back in your home. We'll figure something out."

One time when I ran away I got up the nerve to hitch-hike, rather than walk or take the train. The man who gave me a lift to the city was taken by my story and gave me sixteen rubles. Back in 1988 many people only made about fifteen rubles a month, so this was a lot of money. When I went back home (which, of course, I eventually did), I hid the money, along with some that Valentina had given me, under my mattress.

But my mother found the money. She demanded to know where I got it. When I told her, she didn't believe me and said I had stolen it. Dad went through the same drill when he came home that night. This time the beating was extra severe, the worst I ever received. Sixteen times he beat me with the belt buckle, one for each ruble the man had given me. For the first time, my mother joined in the abuse. Pulling me by the hair, with a knife to my throat, she tied me to a kitchen chair and forced me for several hours to rewrite all of my notebooks. Every time I would make a mistake, she would hit me in the back with a wooden stick. The next morning she sent me to the well to get water. I got the water and put the two buckets on the back porch and then took off.

I had not been able to dress appropriately for the cold weather because to do so would have tipped them off that I was going to bolt again. I was just in shirtsleeves, and I had shoes but no socks. I swore to myself that I would never come back. Desperate, I stole a bicycle and snuck into someone's house and stole a jar of food.

When I finally got to the city, I fell off the bike, exhausted, breaking the jar of jam. I lay down on the park bench, sobbing, hoping that if I lay there long enough, I would freeze to death.

6

*He makes me lie down in green pastures, he leads
me beside quiet waters.*

—Psalm 23:2

I lay on the park bench in St. Petersburg, freezing and
famished, for hours. On and off, I gave into the exhaustion and slept. The next morning a couple came along and
asked me what I was doing. After I shared my story with
them, Misha and Marina kindly took me back to their
apartment, which was only minutes from Orphanage
Number 51.

When Marina helped me take a warm bath, she saw all
of the bruises and welts on my body. She was outraged by
my story and insisted on going to talk with my parents.
As afraid as I was to go back, I went with her to show her
where they lived. On the way we made one stop, to return
the bicycle I had "borrowed."

I refused to go to my parents' door with her; instead I
hid in the bushes. When my father answered her knock on
the door Marina explained who she was and why she was
there, and then entered the home. Not wanting to take
any chances of being discovered, I snuck out of the bushes
and went on down the road to wait for her.

On our train ride back to the city she told me that my
parents denied everything, explaining that I had problems,
not the least of which was my lying. But Marina believed

me; she had seen the evidence. She said that I would stay with them until they figured out what to do.

Marina and Misha were in their mid-fifties. She was a former ballerina and taught ballet. He was an engineer at the Hermitage, the largest museum in Russia and one of the largest and finest in the world. They had lost a child in childbirth and Marina could never bring herself to go through that experience again.

Her first option regarding me was to see if Orphanage 51 would take me back. They would not. Because I had been legally adopted there was nothing they could do. Determined, she went to the city government office that oversaw orphanages and met with the inspector, pleading, "What can we do? He is not safe on the street, not safe at home. The orphanage won't take him. There must be something we can do!" To which they promptly replied, "*Nyet*. There is nothing we can do."

I lived with Marina and Misha for about six months. Their home was a haven for this twelve-year-old misfit who didn't belong anywhere. I did not attend school while I lived with them, as they could not enroll me; so I often stayed home alone while they were at work. Sometimes I went with Marina to the school where she taught ballet. I still remember the stuffed animal—a lion—they gave me, a real treasure to someone who had rarely had anything to call his own. Misha and Marina were both beautiful musicians and I loved to listen to them play the piano. I still keep in touch with them, and call them *tetya* (aunt) and *dyadya* (uncle).

Tetya Marina continued in her determination. She went back to the city inspector and threatened to go to the authorities in Moscow if they didn't do something for me. That seemed to do the trick: Orphanage 51 took me back.

Dyadya Misha and Tetya Marina's apartment:
a refuge in the storm

The orphanage director greeted me with much reluctance and resentment: I was back in the orphanage system, but I wasn't an orphan. While the director did not greet me with enthusiasm, Melana was glad to see me, as were my buddies, Misha and Ed. Irina was still our teacher, and she and Melana had once again secured a sanatorium for our class of twelve-year-olds.

Sunnyville Sanatorium, about twenty minutes north of the other sanatorium, was much bigger. There were twenty-four buildings on the grounds and my class had one section of one of those buildings to ourselves. Each of the buildings had a doctor and a nurse assigned to it, an infirmary, a classroom, and its own dining room.

In our building we had a big playroom and our own bathroom. The bathroom was an improvement—it had both hot *and* cold water—but still no showers. There was one big bedroom for all sixteen of us boys. Our girl classmates had a similar setup.

There was a big closet in our bedroom and each boy had a shelf with his name on it for his clothes. For the first time we were able to wear clothes that belonged to us, rather than clothes that had been mixed up on laundry day. At Sunnyville we did not have to wash our own clothes, we simply took them to the laundry facility once a week. Wednesday was "*banya* day." We would take our clothes and sheets to the laundry and then go to the *banya* or bathhouse, where we would have to wait our turn until after the girls were done. It was an all-day event each week. This being a sanatorium, we also had a regular time referred to as "medical procedures," where we would do our stretching exercises and receive massages. It was a favorite of mine.

While we didn't have to do our laundry, we did have to help out with meals. We took turns running to the kitchen facility with two big buckets that would be filled with our food allotment. There was plenty of play area outside at Sunnyville. There was a big hilly area that was great for sledding. And though a much farther walk than it was from our previous sanatorium, we were still within walking distance from the Bay of Finland where we could play on the beach. Lest you get any wrong ideas of a tropical beach setting, keep in mind that St. Petersburg is as far north as parts of Alaska.

Sunnyville gave me my first opportunity for leadership. Melana assigned me to the *komandir* role for my group, an assistant of sorts to her and Irina. One of my jobs was to make sure all of us had washed and were in bed at bedtime. I took my job very seriously, inspecting my classmates' feet and behind their ears before letting them get in bed. I was also the exercise leader and would lead our group in an exercise regime out on the lawn each morning.

Like lots of kids that age, it was during this time that I experienced my first "love." Sveta was a cute girl a year younger than me. Nothing came of it, but it is a fond memory for me and we remain friends.

One other thing that was special about Sunnyville is that there, for the first time in our young lives, we celebrated birthdays. While there were no elaborate gifts or extravagant parties like kids in America have, Melana felt it was important for each of us to be recognized and have a little celebration on our special day. For us, it was a priceless experience.

For the first time, with my leadership role and my birthday celebration, I began to be recognized as an individual. By all external measures, my life at Sunnyville was the best it had ever been. It could have marked a turning point toward a purposeful life for me. Yet internally I was struggling. Looking back, I know that the Lord was not finished with His process of calling me. The fires of purification were about to get much hotter. If the first sanatorium experience was the calm before the storm, Sunnyville was just a pleasant lull before the avalanche. I was about to enter the worst year of my entire life.

7

For our light and momentary troubles are achieving for us an eternal glory that outweighs them all.

—2 Corinthians 4:17

The doctor who was assigned to us at Sunnyville was Dr. Nina. I became close to her and would often spend my free time helping her out in the infirmary. One day she even sent me to the on-site pharmacy in Building 3 to pick up some medicine for one of the kids. To this day I have no idea why I did what I did, but on the walk back I opened the pill bottle and decided to taste one of the pills. It tasted pretty good. I had another. And another. Before I got back to my building, Building 6, I had taken eight of the pills.

It took me a long time just to walk across the campus from the pharmacy to my building. I laid down on a bench and slept for three hours. When someone finally woke me, chiding me for sleeping on the bench in the middle of the day, I went back to my building, collapsing as soon as I got there. Understandably, that frightened my teacher Irina and my classmates, but by then Dr. Nina had gone home for the day and no one knew about the medicine I had been sent to get. I collapsed at my desk and slept through school that afternoon. When I requested to be excused from dinner and go to bed instead, my teacher became even more alarmed.

I awoke in the middle of the night with a lump in my throat obstructing my breathing and my ability to drink. I was terribly thirsty. When the doctor came in at 9:00 the next morning she immediately knew what was wrong. She called an ambulance and I was taken to the hospital. There, my stomach and blood were cleaned by a series of very uncomfortable processes. It turns out that the child dosage for that medicine was ¼ pill a day and I had swallowed eight of them! I ended up in the hospital for almost a month. They told me later I had come close to dying and that if I had taken even just one more pill, I would not have survived. It was a valuable lesson for me and scared me from ever taking illegal drugs. To this day I am very cautious taking medications of any kind.

While in the hospital, after I began to feel better, I became the nurses' helper. I loved being there and helping take care of the other children. I didn't want to be released. But my erratic behavior was not over. About a week after returning to Sunnyville I got into an ugly fight with the nurse on duty in our building. Her name was Lucine. She was an Armenian woman and all of the children hated her. She was just plain mean to us, and most of us were afraid of her. She was picking on one of the girls and I spoke up to defend her. Lucine lashed out at me. With frustration, hurt, and anger toward Lucine swirling inside me, none of which I had ever confronted or dealt with, it all bubbled to the surface. I don't remember exactly what she said to set me off; whatever it was, though, I had had enough. I grabbed a pair of scissors and yelled, "You leave us alone. You do this again and I'm going to kill you!"

I knew, as the words were leaving my mouth, that I didn't mean it. She had just pushed me too far and in anger I struck back. We children went back to our rooms.

I calmed down and thought everything was fine. What I didn't know was that the nurse immediately reported the incident to my caretaker who, unfortunately, happened to be Irina that week (Irina and Melana were continuing their rotation of duties as they had at the first sanatorium).

Irina concurred with Nurse Lucine that I had "mental problems" and promptly had me committed to a mental hospital.

I was escorted to a big, old building in St. Petersburg with bars on the windows. Children in this institution were classified in one of two categories upon admittance and treated accordingly. One was the straightjacketed, fully drugged approach for children with severe problems. Most of them never left. The other approach was less severe, utilizing some behavior modification drugs while still allowing the child to function as normally as possible. Fortunately, I was in this latter group.

Since work was believed to be the best medicine of all, I didn't have school while I was in this institution. Instead, I spent my days packaging ladies' nylons for the State. I slept in a huge room with fifty beds, and for the entire time I was there was never allowed outside.

I remember sitting on my windowsill, behind the bars, watching—and longing for—the world outside. I spent much of my time lying on my bed, thinking about my life. Life was not making much sense for me. Why was I even alive? What was the purpose of my existence?

When she returned to Sunnyville the next week Melana was angry with Irina. While she agreed that I needed to be punished for threatening the nurse, she did not agree that I had mental problems, much less that I needed to be put in a mental institution. But her hands were tied. At that point she could not protect me or rescue me.

During the time I was in the mental institution, my adoptive mother Larisa was kept informed. After about four months she came and had me released and gave me two choices: I could go back to live with them, or go to the streets. I chose the streets. I lived on the streets for a very short time—a few weeks—before the police caught me and took me back to Orphanage Number 51.

Unfortunately for me, while Melana was still there as a caretaker, she was no longer with our class. I was back "home," but with all new caretakers and teachers who rotated from day to day. The director of Number 51 wanted to send me to a special needs orphanage where I would basically have been locked up for the rest of my life. She resented having to take me back in, since I was legally not an orphan, and would love to have gotten rid of me. Her reasoning for putting me into a special needs facility wasn't so much about my well-being as much as it was that she was fearful of what I might do as a result of my trauma with my parents, my life on the streets, and my recent stay in the mental facility. I'm sure to her I was a bad risk, and one she was tired of.

When Melana heard what the director wanted to do she literally got down on her knees and begged her to reconsider. Once again, Melana was proving good to her promise to protect me from harm that she made on the day she met all of us five years earlier. The director relented, and I was able to once again join my class.

It was a rough adjustment for me. While at some level I was thankful to be taken in by the orphanage, after several years with Melana, life at the sanatoriums, and my six-month interlude with Tetya Marina and Dyadya Misha, I faced, for the first time, the stark reality of life as an orphan. There were no more hugs or kisses or individualized attention and affection, no more birthday parties. I continued my process of introspection I had begun during my months at the mental institution, wondering who I was and what was the purpose in living. I questioned why I had to go through all that I had endured. Most of all, I yearned for purpose. I was fearful of what was to come. I was now thirteen years old and I knew that in a few short years the state system would turn me out on my own. I desperately wanted to cling to hope, but I found nothing within myself with which to muster hope.

At this time in my life I hated men. There was a caretaker at Orphanage 51, Alexander, who struck me once when we were all away at winter camp. I was so enraged I took off on my own and walked back to the orphanage—all thirty miles. I cried much of the way, screaming a vow I made to myself: "I will never let another man touch me ever again!" My emotional and physical state when I arrived back at Orphanage 51 must have garnered some sympathy because they allowed me to stay at the orphanage all by myself, with just the women on security. Or maybe they just didn't know what to do with me. I certainly didn't.

Not long after this I had my first court appearance with my parents to hopefully dissolve the adoption. The court was back in the town where they lived and I was accompanied by a social worker, Konstantin. My parents didn't bother to show up.

Things continued to spiral down. At one point during this dark period of my young life I had just had enough and I took off, running as far and as fast as I could from Orphanage 51. The director reported it to the police. "If you catch him," she said, "don't bother bringing him back here!" When the police did catch me they took me directly to the juvenile delinquent home.

This was a huge building, surrounded by barbed wire fencing, bars on all the windows, and guarded by military. This was the place they housed kids who repeatedly ran away from home—or orphanages. It was also where they put kids who had committed crimes. It was basically a holding ground for kids while the authorities decided what was to be done with you.

There were two sections. For most of the older kids, and those who had committed crimes, it was more like a jail where they were housed in cells. The other section was more like a group home for runaways of all ages, some of whom had committed petty crimes.

Upon my arrival I was placed in the infirmary while they processed me and determined into which section they would put me. I was there for three days. I slept on a wooden bench with no blankets. They would bring me a little food in a small aluminum bowl twice a day. For all of my years in orphanages and all my visits to the police department, this was my first experience at being locked up. It was frightening to say the least.

I had no idea what was going on during those three days. I assumed they were talking with the orphanage director and my legal parents. They surely had access to my records and knowledge of my stay in the mental hospital. I had good reasons to fear the worst. Maybe my time was up and they would lock me away and "throw away the key." In some ways I couldn't blame them.

I was relieved when, at the end of those three days, they moved me into the group home. It had a playroom and a huge bedroom, like the orphanage, with forty or more beds. The toilets were nothing more than holes in the ground—like an outhouse, inside. There were sinks with cold water; no showers. The smells in the place were

Kolya (Melana's husband), Maria, Sveta, Melana, Edik, and me, at the Kozeevas' dacha. This was taken in between my stays at the mental institution and the juvenile home

horrendous. We had police officers for guards. And I was on the "good" side!

Homosexuality was very prevalent in the juvenile delinquent center. The boys told me horrible stories about peeing in the younger boys' mouths after they fell asleep, or worse yet, molesting them. I was so scared to go to sleep at night that I rarely slept.

I endured this for three months. One horrific morning, before the rest of the children were awake, some older boys came to me and stripped me of my clothes. As it happened, Konstantin, the social worker from Orphanage 51, arrived to pick me up, just as I was about to be molested. To this day I have no idea why he was sent there or why I was released, I was just thankful that it happened and that I got out of there when I did.

Back at Number 51 I was introduced to three new caretakers. One of them was a man named Vladimir. He was a father of two grown children and was a choreographer for our dance classes. He was a very artsy man who loved little boys. He never molested anyone that I knew of but always used inappropriate touching. He hated me and Ed, joining in with those who called us "the Aristocrats." He hated the way we dressed, our cleanliness and manners, and the fact that we didn't smoke, drink, or swear like the rest of the boys. It drove him crazy. Vladimir, like so many of my countrymen, was an alcoholic who often came to the orphanage drunk. And he continued to drink while he was at work. He was one of our summer camp directors the next summer and he drank all day, every day, during the weeks we were there.

One night that summer all of the counselors were out on the lake drinking after the kids had gone to bed. We were staying in an old building at the camp that had been around since World War II. It had never been renovated, they just kept adding another coat of paint. The building probably had sixty coats on it.

The counselors came back to the building at about 4:00 a.m. One of them left a cigarette burning by the electric heater. What started as a small spark quickly engulfed the entire house in flames. I heard a woman outside, screaming, "Fire!" One of the counselors ran into our room, shouting for all of us to get outside immediately, telling us to leave everything behind. Fortunately, no one was hurt and everyone escaped. The building—all seven thousand square feet of it—burned to the ground in less than thirty minutes.

Vladimir and his wife came running from their building to the burning building. His wife, who was responsible for the inventory at camp, was screaming, "We must save the mattresses!" In true Soviet style she was more concerned for the mattresses than for the sixty children whose lives had been in danger.

They officially shut down the entire camp after the fire. It was a public facility and most of the children there had parents who paid for them to go to camp. But because Orphanage Number 51 was closed for the summer we were the only kids who remained there for that last month. With only the clothes on our backs, we moved to another building. We spent our last weeks of summer camp cleaning out the burned-out building. A bright spot for us was that the counselors would let us go to the lake and swim each evening after working and getting dirty all day.

One of our counselors was a devout Russian Orthodox. She found out that I was interested in church and began to take me to the old Orthodox church across the lake. It was about an hour's walk for us since we had to go clear around the lake. I enjoyed going to church once again for the first time in several years. One Sunday as we walked, she challenged me to be a spiritual leader to the other orphans and she asked me if I would like to meet with the pastor to discuss my becoming a *kroystniy otetz* ("godfather"). I eagerly agreed.

I met with the *batushka* (as priests in the Russian Orthodox Church are known) and he informed me that to become a "godfather" I needed to lead others to baptism. He told me that it was my responsibility to talk to the other orphans about the importance of baptism and he gave me a little prayer book. Like many liturgical denominations, in the Russian Orthodox Church the members do not pray their own prayers, they read and memorize written prayers. The *batushka* told me to bring some kids the following Friday night so they could confess their sins and then they would be baptized on Sunday. I took my assignment very seriously. I selected thirteen kids and persuaded them to come for confession and baptism at the appointed time.

Shortly after the baptism we left camp and all returned to Orphanage 51. I continued to take my role as "godfather" seriously and felt it was my job to make sure my "godchildren" grew spiritually, even though I really had no idea what that meant.

Tanya, one of my thirteen "godchildren" and a class-mate, was a social orphan. Her mother was an alcoholic and her father was handicapped. The father retained legal rights even though the mother's parental rights had been revoked. Tanya lived at the orphanage because her father could not care for her. She did, however, get to go home for visits on the weekends.

One Monday she didn't show up at Number 51 after her weekend visit. When the caretakers called her home, Tanya's father said that she had taken the bus to return to the orphanage that morning.

It was two weeks later that they found her body. It was in a culvert by the highway. She had been raped and stabbed ten times. By the time they found her, animals had gotten to her body. Tanya's best friend Sveta (my first "love") had to go down and identify the body. Even though there wasn't much left of her to identify, Sveta knew her by her hands and the little ring on her finger.

I went to a Russian Orthodox church in the city that night and lit a candle for Tanya's salvation, a tradition in the church. The church refused to do a memorial service for her because she was an orphan. I felt the weight of the world upon me. I felt that the other kids would be looking to me for spiritual leadership, for comfort, and for peace amidst their anguish, but inside I knew that I had nothing to offer them.

Our entire class went to the cemetery. Because she was an orphan she had to be buried outside the city. We had to escort her body there ourselves. We carried the casket out from the morgue, put it on the bus with us, and rode with her on the long journey to her grave.

My classmates all stood around the grave and looked to me in bewilderment. I laid a candle on her casket and said the Lord's Prayer, the only thing I could think to say at the time. I was broken up by Tanya's murder, but I was also heartbroken to realize that I had failed everyone as a spiritual leader. For all its ritual and "spirituality," my religion had nothing to offer me when I needed it most, and I in turn had nothing to offer to the others. I turned my back on the Russian Orthodox Church that day, and accelerated my journey into darkness, despair, and hopelessness.

About that same time, one of our classmates, Sasha, was adopted. Even though we never talked about adoption or even thought about it much (and after my experience, I certainly never wanted to think about it again), it hit all of us pretty hard. It was not just difficult to lose one of our "family," but also to realize that he now had a family and we didn't. Within days of Sasha's leaving with his new family, the parents of one of the girls in our class got their parental rights back and came to take her home again.

I should have been happy for those kids, yet I wasn't. It just made me more sad and depressed. To make matters worse, my friend Misha (who was also a social orphan, with a single mom) got word that his mother was found dead in her apartment. She had been dead for almost a month before they found her. Misha took it very hard. Yet again I found myself with no words of comfort or answers for a grieving friend. Like me, Misha was now a true orphan.

I became a real loner. I found myself crying uncontrollably all the time. One "disco night" at Number 51, while everyone else was dancing and having a good time, I ran up onto the stage and rolled myself into the curtain and just cried. I spent a lot of time alone in my room, contemplating, reflecting, wondering. I felt hopeless. I saw no purpose in living. I remember thinking, "Why was I born? What's the point?" The orphanage was by a river and I would often sit on the embankment just to be alone to think and cry. It was there at the river's edge that I began contemplating how to end my life. I thought about how I would go about drowning myself. I tried choking myself with my own hands, and one time with a rope, but I would pass out before I could successfully end my life.

My guardian angels were working overtime that year. I had spent a month in the hospital for the accidental drug overdose. Within weeks of that I had spent four months in the mental institution. Then, although reunited with my classmates at Orphanage 51, I had lost Melana's regular presence in my life. Before the twelve months were over I spent another three months in the juvenile delinquent home. While I soared rather quickly to the height of "spiritual leader" for my fellow orphans, I came crashing down just as quickly. My "religion," as everything else in my life, had failed me; when I needed it most it wasn't there for me. No amount of remembering or reflecting upon the rituals could bring a single ounce of comfort or understanding to my heart and mind.

It was, without a doubt, the worst year of my life. I have heard it said that thirteen is the age when most people begin to ask the big questions of life. Whether it was my age, or the culmination of circumstances that I faced that year, or (most likely) both, it was my first real experience with introspection.

For the first time in my life I recognized my need for identity, for purpose, for love, and for hope. And taking full stock of my life at that time, I found myself desperately void of all. Life, I found, was not worth living.

8

And how can they preach unless they are sent? As it is written, "How beautiful are the feet of those who bring good news!"

—Romans 10:15

In the midst of all the turmoil in my own life, the Soviet Union collapsed in 1991. Not even fourteen yet, I did not really grasp the significance, but almost immediately my comrades and I began to feel the effects of this historic event. Very soon after the collapse, new orphanages opened. Where Number 51 used to house five hundred to six hundred orphans, there were now only about one hundred fifty of us.

Because of our reputation for being different from most of the other orphans, Ed and I were given our own room. For us, this was heaven. Our life's purpose became tending to our new home. We would polish the floors every day. With the downsizing of the orphanage, we were able to borrow miscellaneous pieces of now unused furniture. We had our own sofa in our room and even acquired our own television set! We had a cupboard with glass doors that we began to fill with all of our earthly treasures. Our little stuffed animals were relegated to the cupboard, never again to be played with or slept with, but rather, displayed and admired. We even lined our windowsill with plants.

Of course we made our beds every day and washed our linens and clothes with our usual disciplined regularity. If we were going to carry the moniker of "the Aristocrats," we might as well fulfill that role to the best of our ability.

Vladimir, the alcoholic caretaker, hated us even more because of our obvious elitism. The orphanage director, however, seized the opportunity and capitalized on our efforts. Whenever government officials or foreign guests came to Orphanage Number 51 she would use our room to demonstrate how nice the rooms were in her orphanage. (Of course, the doors to the other kids' rooms remained under lock and key during those visits and inspections.)

In his fury, Vladimir was eventually able to confiscate our television, but he couldn't take away our space. Ed and I lived together in our own room from 1992 to 1995. Just as the shattering globe from the chandelier on our first day at Orphanage 51 was an ominous symbol of what was about to happen during the next several years, so this little piece of heaven that Ed and I created in our last years at the orphanage was probably symbolic. We were beginning, in ever so small and seemingly insignificant ways, to make our marks as individuals within the system. For the first time in our lives we had some control over our circumstances.

Not all of the immediate changes after the collapse were improvements for us orphans. About thirty percent of the State sponsorship of the orphanages was dropped. Basic supplies, food, and some clothing were supplied by the State, but it was now up to each orphanage to secure sponsors to help with other expenses and needs. We no longer had free access to the Houses of Culture or free passes to the movie house. We also no longer had "new clothes day" where we were issued our three new sets of uniform clothing for the year. Now, we might be lucky enough to get one new set of state-issued clothing. And since my classmates and I were now fourteen years old and growing every day this was a particular problem for us! We now had to depend on donations of used clothing. (One side benefit to this is that we no longer were able to all dress alike, a welcome change.) We no longer had access to the sanatoriums and our summer camp experiences were devoid of the many recreational programs we used to have.

Some things improved over time. Dental care was a great example. When I was growing up, before the collapse, dental care was almost nonexistent. The only time I ever saw a dentist was when I complained of a toothache. For that cavity the treatment consisted of two people holding me down while a dentist drilled my tooth—without any anesthetic. It was not uncommon that while drilling and trying to hold down the patient the dentist would end up cracking the tooth, at which point they would just pull the tooth—also without anesthetic. I lost four of my permanent teeth in that manner. (Fortunately, since being in the United States I have had excellent care, without which I might be toothless. At age eighteen I got five root canals and seventeen fillings. It took about a year for my initial restoration, followed years later by orthodontic work.) Today, the orphanages have access to very nice dental clinics with money from the West, and many churches send dentists to the orphanages who donate their time and talent on missions trips.

After the collapse the borders of Russia were opened for the first time. I remember the very first time we received a shipment from "the outside." It was a crate of the biggest, sweetest, juiciest apples we had ever seen or tasted. They were from a family in Holland. Later, we received a crate of supplies—including clothes—from a church in Finland. It was the first time we received clothes that were not from Russia. Russian clothes were always drab and in dark colors. We were excited about the "new," colorful clothing. It didn't matter a bit to us that they were secondhand.

When one missionary sponsor from the United States sent a huge, forty-ton container of supplies to Orphanage 51 in 1991, an unfortunate practice ensued that continues to this day. There was so much stuff in that shipment that it became a part-time job for the kids to inventory and store the goods. It took about two months to get it all inventoried and put away. Meanwhile, the orphanage workers were hauling out stuff in duffle bags every night. To this day, much of what is donated to the orphanages ends up in the apartments of the workers, rather than in the hands of the orphans.

The most significant change, however, had nothing to do with supplies or clothing; it had to do with people. For the first time, Russia was open to foreign visitors. I remember the very first visitors at Orphanage 51. They were from Finland. They brought with them donations of colorful clothes and food items. They also brought guitars with them, which we had never seen, and they did a whole performance for us, singing and sharing about Jesus. I was not overly impressed with their message of a loving, caring God who had a plan for our lives. I saw no real value to the message when my own experiences had taught me otherwise. Nonetheless, I was thrilled with their visit and the performance and, moreover—for the first time in my life—seeing people filled with joy and purpose. It had a lasting effect on me.

Three of the folks from the group—Leena, the leader,

and a married couple named Erkki and Salme—became the first foreigners that I ever met. They asked for special permission to take me out of the orphanage and I joined them as they went to minister to the special needs orphanage—the same one I was almost sent to. I got a glimpse of what my life could have been like had it not been for Melana's pleading on my behalf. It was extremely depressing, but it was a good experience for me.

I kept in touch with Erkki and Salme after they left. We had a speech pathologist at the orphanage and she translated for me as we exchanged letters. Every time they came back to Russia I got permission to join them on their mission trips to other orphanages.

My first court hearing with my adoptive parents was when I was thirteen and they failed to show up for the hearing. I was fourteen before the second hearing was scheduled. Again, they did not show. It was almost a year later before the third hearing and this time my parents did appear. What we were all expecting was just a legal dissolution of the parent/child relationship, but the judge first asked each of us to tell what happened.

I did not intend for it to happen, but, with tears streaming down my face, I told the entire story—the abuse, the drinking, the running away, all of it. The judge was appalled. She then stated that this was no longer just a civil case, that she needed to open a criminal investigation. Of course, my parents denied everything. But then, in front of the judge, they also threatened to kill me. The judge wanted to put Kolya in jail for four years. The judge's attitude was another change brought about by the collapse of the Soviet Union. During the Soviet time nobody cared—not the police, not the juvenile authorities, not the courts. Now you have officials who really care. This particular judge was not only suggesting jail time for Kolya, but also that my parents pay me child support until I was eighteen.

Even I was surprised when I pleaded mercy for them. But it wasn't my parents for whom I felt compassion, but their daughter Maria. I did not want her to be fatherless. I also didn't want anything from them, not even money. I just wanted to be done with them and to have my name back and to have my legal orphan status reinstated. The judge granted my requests. Officially, I had been considered a homeless child for four years and no one had legal responsibility for me, even though I had been back in the orphanage system.

Now, at fifteen, I was once again a legal orphan. That last court appearance marked the end of my relationship with my adoptive parents. It was also through the process of this hearing that all of my records were lost, with the exception of my medical records, which were still held at Orphanage Number 51.

My failed adoption had been a devastating emotional experience for me. Inside I was angry, sad, and broken. More than that, I was afraid. I was not only afraid of all men, I was afraid that I would never again be able to trust anyone. I had several more offers in later years to be adopted by other Russian families, but I refused them all. I was afraid of being abused again. I broke down and cried like a baby in front of the judge on the day of that final hearing. My emotions were still raw from the experience, even four years after leaving my adopted home.

The only adults with whom I felt safe were Melana and Irina. Whether it was guilt after sending me to the mental institution or, more likely, Melana's influence over the years, Irina came around to being very loving and kind to me and Ed. She would even hug and kiss us, and had us to her home for meals sometimes. I'm sorry we didn't have that relationship when she was our caretaker and teacher.

That same year, American missionaries also came to the orphanage. It was the first time in my life I had ever met an American. They were Jim and Sherry Oxendine and they came with their church group from Tennessee. They happened to come on my fifteenth birthday, December 6, 1992. Sherry came with a bag of gifts for all the kids and presented an individual gift to each child. I received a wallet. It seemed like the happiest day of my life.

Sherry became a special friend. She promised me that she would come back, and she did, three times a year. On each visit she would spend special time with me. Since her birthday was near mine, we would celebrate our birthdays together. She would take me to restaurants—a new experience for me—and take me on tours around St. Petersburg, a far cry from when I wandered the streets alone as a child.

But Sherry had a more important motivation than just giving me good memories. She shared the good news of God's love for me through Christ. She told me how much God loved me and that He was waiting for me to give my heart to Him and follow Him. She caused me to really think about this more carefully and seriously.

At one point she and Jim talked to me about adopting me. I was thrilled; not just because I really liked them, but because they were Americans. The talk and the process went on for over a year. When I was sixteen I found out that it wasn't going to happen. I never did find out what caused the Oxendines to change their minds. They had become financial sponsors of the orphanage and I know that the orphanage director did not want the adoption to go through. She was afraid they would lose their biggest sponsor if they adopted a Russian orphan and went home.

I broke down when I got the news. I did not take it well. My dreams of America and a family were crushed in one blow. Along with sharing her faith with me, Sherry had also been instrumental in beginning to teach me English. She encouraged me to continue learning and to come to the United States one day. She also challenged me to think about my future and to set goals over the years. These were new concepts to me.

The Oxendines moved to Moscow in 1997 to continue their work with Russian orphanages and I have kept in touch with them. In 1999, a few years after I had been on my own, Sherry brought a team of young people from America to Orphanage 51 to do a renovation project. I was able to help them for two weeks of very hard labor, a very rewarding and meaningful project for me.

The Lord definitely used Sherry to sew some new seeds in my heart and, maybe, for the first time, to begin to look to the future instead of the past.

9

*He said to them, "Go into all the world and preach
the good news to all creation."*
                                                    —Mark 16:15

The influx of foreigners into Russia, and specifically
into the orphanage, was a huge change for us. It literally changed my life. Almost immediately after the collapse of the Soviet Union, a delegation from the Ministry
of Education and Science flew to the United States and
gave personal invitations to eighty different Christian
organizations to come to Russia to help lead a spiritual
revival. After seventy-five years of Christianity being officially forbidden, this was a big deal. One of those ministries was The Navigators, an evangelistic ministry with an
emphasis on discipleship.

All of us orphans enjoyed the visitors, especially those
bearing gifts. More than any of my peers, however, I was
intrigued by the foreigners, and most of all, the Americans.
Like most Russians, I was fascinated by all things American. We had been told all of our lives that the United States
was bad, and only bad stuff came from it. But regardless of
what the Soviet system fed us in school, we also knew that
it was the land of opportunity—much better than Russia
or any of the former Soviet republics. In those early days I
admit that my attraction to Americans was purely selfish.
I was sure that somehow they could do something for me

to improve my life, to better my circumstances. Therefore, I took every chance I was given to speak with the Americans, to seek them out and get to know them.

I found out that there were four Americans living in an apartment near Number 51. I just had to meet them. Speaking no English, and only fourteen years old at the time, I mustered up my courage and knocked on the door of the apartment.

Speaking no Russian, they still welcomed me into their home. I really connected with one of the men, Lloyd. Over the next three months or so, I would visit with Lloyd two or three times a week. Through translators, I learned that they were part of a preparation team for The Navigators. The Colorado Springs-based ministry was planning a larger effort in St. Petersburg, called a Co-Mission, and they were getting things ready for it.

When the time came for Lloyd and the team to go back to the States I knew that I would never see him again. I was very sad. It felt like another betrayal. But Lloyd said, "I promise that when the first Co-Mission team comes to St. Petersburg, I will make sure that they come to Orphanage Number 51 to meet you."

True to his promise, a few months later a huge group of Americans came to Orphanage 51 for a tour. As they were about to leave, one of them asked, "Where is Alex Krutov?"

Through a translator, they explained that they were part of the team from The Navigators. The Navigator team, in turn, was part of a larger group of some fifty or sixty missionaries with more than twenty translators. A lot of the missionaries settled into apartments in the downtown area of St. Petersburg, close to the orphanage.

Once again, I took it upon myself to seek out the Americans. Something—or Someone—was drawing me to spend time with these people. There were three new Americans living in the apartment where Lloyd had lived, including a man named Doug Jester. I not only had a new American friend, Doug, but also a translator, Constantine, who was from the Russian military and did translating on the side. (How much had things changed in so little time! A Russian military man translating for an American Christian ministry in St. Petersburg would have been a treasonous activity only a few years earlier. But Russia was changing fast.) With Constantine's help, I was really able to communicate with my new friend.

I began going to Doug's apartment three or four times a week during my free time. We talked for hours about my life and the pain I had experienced. We read Scripture together. It was the first time I had ever opened God's Word for myself. This went on for about six months, and it was during this catharsis that I first began to understand the concept of a God who loved and cared for me.

Whenever Doug was out of the room, however, Constantine took every opportunity to scold me. "Shut up and stop whining about your life!" It was at this point that I vowed to start learning English for myself so I would never have to depend on a translator again. I would sit quietly on the couch of the Americans' apartment and intently listen to their conversations, trying to pick out vocabulary. I grilled the Americans for definitions and pronunciations. Once I started learning words, I would ask them to help me put together sentences. I didn't want them to make fun of me, but I gave them permission to correct my attempts to speak their language. Slowly but surely, with slightly "broken" English, I began to communicate with my new friends on my own.

One Sunday Doug invited me to attend church with

him at the International Church of St. Petersburg. The church had been started by missionaries and probably half of the congregation were foreign missionaries from all over the world. The church was meeting in one of the Houses of Culture buildings. I remember being greeted by ladies at the door, who shook my hand and welcomed me to their church. I was amazed to see so many people carrying their own Bibles, and even more surprised to hear the congregation singing praises. It was a far cry from my former church experience. In the Orthodox Church no one had their own Bible and only the choir did the singing. Devoid of any fancy building or elaborate rituals that I associated with church, there was nonetheless something very attractive in this body of believers who called themselves a church. I began to go every Sunday with Doug.

Some of the American influence on the orphans was more tangible. With the influx of Western money and American sponsors, Orphanage Number 51 got showers with hot water. You would think that kids would be lining up each day for hot showers, or at the very least, every week. Not so. I guess if you aren't used to something—if you don't grow up with it—it's just not a priority. I had always been more inclined to personal cleanliness than most of my peers, but now that I was around the Americans so much of the time I became very motivated to step up my hygiene game. I welcomed my hot shower every morning. Since the orphans had a tendency to destroy things, the nice, new shower rooms were kept under lock and key. On Sundays I had to get up before 7:00 to make it to church. I was given special permission to have a key so I could take my early Sunday morning showers.

I would go to Doug's apartment for breakfast (where I discovered hot chocolate!), then we would go to church, and often to lunch with others after the service. Sundays became the highlight of my week.

After about six months of attending this church with my American friends, the pastor, an American missionary from California, gave an invitation for folks to come forward at the close of the service and accept Christ into their lives. My heart was stirred. But I did not want this to just be a mental decision. I somehow felt that if I walked forward and said a prayer to accept Christ it would be a transaction that only involved my head, and not my heart. I knew that if I was going to do this I needed it to be more. Though I had begun to ask eternally significant questions when I was thirteen, it was only now, as I had just turned sixteen, that I was able to understand the answers to those questions. I was desperately seeking someone who would *never* leave me. I looked deep into Doug's eyes and told him that I didn't want to walk down to the stage, but that I wanted to accept Christ.

Doug shared a Bible verse with me as I sat beside him: "I will not leave you orphans; I will come to you" (John 14:18). With Doug praying beside me, I accepted Christ that Sunday in December 1993, first as my heavenly *Father*, then as my Savior.

I got even more involved with The Navigators and the church. While my new life with my American friends and their church was very exciting to me, life at "home" had not changed. If anything, it was worse. Everyone at Orphanage 51 came to realize that I was more involved with the Americans and their church than I was with anything at the orphanage and many of them hated and resented me for that. The English teacher in the orphanage resented the fact that I could speak the language better than she could. Others felt that I was a deserter who was betraying my own country. One of the caretakers came up to me and said, "You mark my word. The day will come when you will come to me on hands and knees and beg me for bread and water when your American friends are gone—and I won't give it to you!"

The summer of 1994 was a lonely time for me. At camp that summer, I didn't fit in anymore. At sixteen, I was no longer a child, and my affiliation with the American Christians set me apart from the others. So I spent most of that summer working on special projects around the camp, and spent more time with the counselors than the kids, and the counselors were drunk most of the time. My roommate was a seventeen-year-old boy named Dima. He hated me and physically abused me. He, too, was often drunk, which only heightened his anger towards me. One night, however, his drunkenness almost certainly protected me. As I lay sleeping in my bed, Dima came in, drunk as usual. He came at me with a powerful punch aimed for my face. But because of his drunken stupor, he missed my face and slammed his fist into the wooden headboard of the bed, splitting it down the middle.

Summer camp took me away from my time with the missionaries and the church for three months. I began to ponder my decision to trust Christ with my life and sometimes questioned it. Is there really a loving God? Why can't I feel His presence or hear His voice except when I am with the American Christians? Is this "personal relationship with Christ" for real? I even contemplated, once again, taking my own life. While I never again attempted it, I still cried a lot that summer and spent hours alone, desperately seeking assurance.

The first day back at Orphanage 51, after camp, I was sitting at the table eating when Dima walked by and spit in my food. While I was no match for Dima in size or strength, I had had enough. I took off after him and shoved him to the ground. Fearing his response, I beat a hasty retreat. He took off after me and the next thing I knew, his foot came flying up and hit me square in the back, sending me crashing down, sliding across the granite floor.

I was taken to the trauma room, and fortunately nothing was broken. I called my old friend Valentina at the police department. She was the police captain now, but had been the Inspector for Youth Rights during my runaway days. Over the past several years I had run into her several times and had even, on occasion, stopped to visit with her at the station. Apart from Melana in my younger years, Valentina had been my most consistent protector. She came out to the orphanage and had a talk with Dima.

"If you ever touch this boy again, you'll have to answer to me. I have enough in your case file to make your life miserable!" she said, all the while jabbing a finger in Dima's chest. He never touched me again.

Back in 1987 Mikhail Gorbachev had made a law that each Russian orphan would get a monthly allowance. It amounted to only a few American dollars, but for us that was a lot of money. Melana and Irina used our money to buy extra things for us, like birthday gifts. It wasn't until we were older that we started receiving our monthly allowance ourselves. Most of the kids used their money for alcohol and cigarettes, both of which were cheap and there was no law restricting their purchase by minors. Some of the kids used their money to purchase drugs. Ed and I used our money to buy things like deodorant and shampoo. Our big luxury was "Ring," a Russian cologne. When the other kids would run out of money for their alcohol, they would sneak into our room and drink a capful of our cologne.

Not long after my incident with Dima, the old school-house attached to Orphanage Number 51 was shut down. Now housing fewer orphans, the configuration of living space was changed. New walls and doors were put up, making for smaller rooms. The fourth floor that once housed only the boys was now divided into two sections, separated by a wall, with a number of smaller bedrooms in each section, some for the girls and some for the boys. Somehow Ed and I, still with our own personal room, ended up on the side with the younger, fifth, sixth, and seventh graders.

This seemingly random decision proved to be a huge blessing in my life. Ed and I were not exposed to all that happened on the other side of the fourth floor. Besides the usual smoking and drinking and drugs, the boys began sleeping with the girls. One of the girls, aged fourteen, became pregnant and was rather suddenly transferred to another orphanage. There was also a lot of homosexual behavior, not just among the boys themselves, but also the male caretakers molesting some of the boys. It was sad for me to see how much my class was falling apart. Most of my classmates had made a mess of their lives. Admittedly, though, I also felt very thankful to be protected and separated from them.

Conversely, because we were the oldest of the orphans on our side of the wall, we became surrogate caretakers for the younger kids. We knew from our own experience the value of a loving caregiver and it became our mission to provide that for the young orphans.

Years later I learned that Orphanage Number 51 was designated for orphans with "mental learning disability." That was just a classification for children with slow development due to lack of parenting, nutrition, or nurture. Many of the orphans had suffered as babies from fetal alcohol syndrome, for instance, but they were not mentally retarded. We did, however, have one little girl who was mentally handicapped.

In 1992 we had the first black child come to Orphanage Number 51, a young boy. One day his teacher left the classroom for a time to have tea, or possibly a drink, with her colleagues. While she was away from the class four of the children decided to go down to the river. Among them was the black boy. As the children sat on the riverbank, dangling their feet in the water, "the crazy girl," as the children called the mentally handicapped girl, suddenly came up behind them and pushed the little black boy into the river. Another girl jumped in to try to save him, but the current was strong that fall and she soon found herself in trouble.

Her screams solicited help from passersby. While they were successful in rescuing the little girl from the water, there was no sign of the boy. It took the authorities eight hours to find his little body, almost seven miles downstream.

Nina, one of the caretakers, contacted the morgue and the cemetery. When they found out that the child was not only an orphan but also a black boy, she was told they had no caskets available for him. It took her two or three days to locate one—a six-foot casket for a seven-year-old boy. The cemetery, again outside the city, agreed to dig a grave but told the orphanage that we would have to bury him ourselves. I will never forget that day, as we all stood there, using sticks because we had no shovels, trying to move enough dirt to cover the very large casket.

The teacher, who had neglected her classroom, was re-moved from Orphanage Number 51 but there were never any charges brought against her.

There was another little boy that winter who ran away from the orphanage. Tired and cold, he laid down under a parked bus to sleep. The bus driver had no idea the boy was there and ran over him, crushing him to death.

Over a ten-year period I knew of at least ten children from Orphanage Number 51 who died. I point this out be-cause orphans were dispensable. No one really cared about the death of an orphan, and no one was ever charged with negligence or liability for such "accidents."

I continued to go to church and Bible studies, but my newfound faith in Christ was fragile at best. One day just before my seventeenth birthday there was another inci-dent at Orphanage 51 that shook me up, but it also served to strengthen my faith. I was outside the orphanage talk-ing to my friend Maria, when an eighteen-year-old, for no good reason, threw a large glass bottle full of water out of the fourth floor window, aimed directly at my head. I happened to move at just the right moment and the bottle crashed to the ground in front of me, shattering into a million pieces. That incident made a deep impression on me as I contemplated what could have happened if I had not moved just when I did.

Shortly after the bottle incident I met Sam and Pam Rhine from The Navigators' team. I shared the story with them. In turn, they shared Jeremiah 29:11 with me. "'For I know the plans that I have for you,' declares the Lord, 'plans to prosper you and not to harm you, plans to give you a hope and a future.'"

With the seemingly random bottle incident in my mind and that Bible verse on my heart, my faith took hold.

From that point on, I never again considered ending my life. Rather, my whole life became focused on discovering what plans and future my heavenly Father had for me.

Sam and Pam Rhine lived in a large apartment near Number 51 and I began inviting friends from my side of the fourth floor, including the younger kids, to join me at the Rhines' home. We would have play time, cookie and tea time, and then Bible study time. The kids loved it.

My English was getting better, but not well enough to serve as a translator, so there would be translators there. My new friends, my new faith, and my new language were all converging together to offer me a new life.

The Navigators were on a short-term rotation. Doug Jester had left just after he led me to Christ, and when Sam and Pam Rhine left, Bob and Rita Lyon came to take their place. The Lyons had two little girls, Molly, age three, and Lisa, age seven. Being around all the various missionaries and now around a missionary family, my attitude toward Americans began to change. I began to think less about what they could do for me, and to think more about the sacrifices they were making. I began to feel very appreciative of their work.

The Lyons expressed an interest in adoption; not of me, but of a fourteen-year-old in Orphanage 51, named Galya. A year later, the adoption went through. This was only the second foreign adoption from our orphanage, and this time, instead of feeling sad or jealous, I was excited for both the Lyons and Galya.

As my English improved I became a tour guide for many of the Navigator teams that were in St. Petersburg. I welcomed the opportunity to make a little money, see the city, and get out of the orphanage. I also began relationships with dozens of American Christians.

Some of the missionary families began to ask me to babysit for them. I also became a "gofer" of sorts, running errands for the missionaries. It made me feel important to be delivering documents to government buildings and to be dining at nice restaurants with the various missionaries. My life was vastly different in 1993 and 1994, primarily because of the ministry of The Navigators in St. Petersburg. I will forever be grateful.

The summer camps of those years were also vastly different. Vladimir had been fired as the camp director, and one of our caretakers at Number 51, Nina, was the new camp director. We were at a new camp now, one owned by one of the State's factories. Most camps do not want the older orphans—too many problems with drinking, smoking, and drugs. But there were a lot of kids at this camp who were not orphans. Their parents paid for them to come to camp for a couple of weeks in the summer. There were new kids rotating into the camp every fourteen days, all summer long.

Nina got permission to bring some of us from Number 51 to this camp. (In a welcome change, they no longer had one orphanage to a camp, but instead mixed up the orphanages and sent some from each orphanage to different camps.) I was fortunate to get assigned to Nina's camp. She decided she wanted to make camp really nice for us, so she invited American missionaries to join us. With funds from the missionaries, she fixed up the camp. The first thing she did was add a *banya* with hot water.

The missionaries would do Bible studies, lead singing, bring treats, and do arts and crafts with the kids, much like vacation Bible schools in the States. They also performed skits and concerts for us. It was very resourceful on Nina's part to do this. The kids loved those summer camps. The various mission groups that came during the summer would invariably only have one translator, so I got to serve as a second translator. That's all I did, all day, every day, and I loved it.

One day I was talking to a librarian at the camp and she was asking me about the missionaries and "all this spiritual stuff." I got to personally share my faith for the first time. While she didn't respond the way I wanted her to, it was a milestone for me, not only in learning to share my faith, but also in the realization that faith is a matter of choice. It wasn't my place to make someone else believe.

Though 1993 was a year of great beginnings for me, it was not so good for Melana. Our former caretaker and surrogate mother lost her beloved father. A few months after that she and her husband went to their *dacha* to collect their summer harvest. They were awakened in the middle of the night as their German shepherd was barking incessantly. They discovered that the *dacha* was on fire. In only a matter of minutes everything was destroyed. Then, worst of all, a few weeks later her husband fell from a crane at a construction site and was killed. Before the year was over, Melana herself had a stroke and was paralyzed and hospitalized for months. All of us in my class were heartbroken for our dear friend and protector.

Despite all of the positive changes in my own life, I had not begun to experience any real inner healing. I had yet to deal with any of my past. Having spent most of my life focused on past hurts and disappointments, I was much too eager to get on with my new life to think about what lay behind. I was especially excited to discover God's plan for my future. Dealing with the other stuff would have to wait.

CLASS PHOTO
This of course is not my entire class. Many simply did not show up for the photo. In the back row, that's me, Edik, Marina, and Oleg. In the front row are Sveta, Nelly Viktorovan (our caretaker at the time), Marina, and Zhenya. This was taken after Melana was no longer our caretaker. Unfortunately there is no date on the photo, but I believe I was about fourteen or fifteen at the time

10

In his heart a man plans his course, but the Lord determines his steps.

—Proverbs 16:9

The Navigators, in many respects, became my family. At one point, through Doug Jester, my original Navigator contact, I met Mel and Mary Lou Duke. They headed up the St. Petersburg team. Whereas regular team members were in Russia for one year, the Dukes were there for five. While Mary Lou spoke some Russian and I was learning English, mostly we relied on a translator to communicate with one another. In the early nineties we were really just acquaintances; they were very kind people, like so many others that the Lord brought into my life at that time. Later they would come to play a more significant role.

The same could be said for Sue Gregg. One Sunday when the pastor invited folks to stand and greet those around them, Mary Lou Duke introduced me to her friend of more than twenty years, Sue Gregg. Sue was not on The Navigators staff, she was a volunteer with an unusual job. Many of the missionary teams had experienced health problems related to diet issues while they were in Russia. Before the fast food/grocery store influence of the West hit my country, our food was very different. We didn't use cookbooks or recipes or even measurements.

We ate a lot of grains that would have been foreign to Americans, in particular millet (what Americans think of as birdseed) and buckwheat (associated in America with pancake flour). Cooked buckwheat in a bowl with butter and sugar is served for a breakfast dish like oatmeal is in the States—I still prepare it sometimes, even when I am in America. That same buckwheat grain would be cooked, then fried in a skillet with onions and spices for dinner. There was no lettuce or broccoli in Russia at that time. A green salad was considered an exotic American dish, foreign food to us. (A culinary side note: We had never heard of peanut butter in the Soviet Union. Every time a new mission team came they brought jars and jars of the stuff with them in their suitcases.)

Probably ninety-five percent of our spices had never been heard of by the Westerners. We had only instant coffee, no slow-roasted coffee beans like the Americans wanted. We Russians drank a lot of tea, and we ate bread with every meal. We also ate a lot of cabbage and potatoes. What we called potato salad was not like American potato salad at all, it was just potatoes and sausage served cold.

The *dachas* were more than just vacation homes. They were places people escaped the city to grow their own food. Folks would grow their own fruits and vegetables and can them. If folks didn't have a *dacha* they would buy canned goods from those who did.

Sue Gregg is an expert in nutritious cooking, and she and her husband have a nutritional cookbook business. Mary Lou Duke invited her longtime friend to join the Navigators group in St. Petersburg and her mission was to help teach the missionary families how to cook and eat in Russia, using foods readily available, and still stay healthy. This particular visit when I met Sue was her first time to the former Soviet Union. Though we only met briefly on that trip, it was a seed that God planted in my life that would come to fruition in the coming years.

Many people have asked me if it was a cultural shock for me when I finally came to the United States. It wasn't. I had spent so much time with the Americans in Russia those last few years in the orphanage that I had gotten to know the American personality and culture in many respects.

Most Russians think all Americans are very wealthy. Even the missionaries living in Russia lived a much better life than most of the people they were ministering to. (Little did I know how much they had sacrificed to be there!) When I compared their lives to mine in Russia, I knew one thing: I wanted to go to America. I had no idea how that could ever come about or what I would do once I got there, but I knew in my heart that my future was somehow in the United States, not Russia.

I also knew that my future was looming. In Russia when an orphan graduates he is put out of the orphanage. I was seeing what was happening to older orphans who had graduated and it was disturbing. Most of them ended up on the street, into drugs, alcohol, prostitution, or crime.

Normal Russian education consists of eleven grades. In the orphanages we only got nine grades of what was considered basic education. Because we did not have the full eleven years, orphan graduates could not attend universities for higher education. There was an option for us called PTUs that we could go to: three- or four-year programs that consisted of finishing the high school diploma plus a year or two of trade school. The State provided these without charge. There were a few hundred PTUs in St. Petersburg alone. Public school students could select what trade school they wanted to attend. Orphans were

assigned by the government to whatever PTUs had availability; not surprisingly, these were often the ones that
no one wanted. These PTUs included dormitory housing. While in concept this might sound pretty good, and
certainly sounds like a good next step for orphans, the
dormitories there were even worse than those at the orphanages. Most orphans in the Russian system have no
self-discipline, study skills, life skills, or motivation. Very
few of them go on to the trade schools.

While Russian orphans leave the orphanage system at
age seventeen or eighteen they remain legal wards of the
State until age twenty-three. For true orphans who opt not
to go to school at a PTU, the government is supposed to
offer them a room in a communal apartment. The social
orphans, while also still legally wards of the State until age
twenty-three, are required to go back to their parent or
parents—the same ones who were deemed unqualified to
be parents in the first place. Generally, the parents are still
alcoholics, still abusive; nothing has changed. So, most orphans don't go back. They would rather live on the streets.
Sometimes they bunk with a true orphan who got a flat,
which means you often see six or seven kids in a one-room
apartment.

Jobs were very scarce back then. It was only a few years
after the collapse of the Soviet Union and most of the jobs
were state jobs, which you could not get without having
had military service.

St. Petersburg has more communal apartments than
anywhere else in Russia and they were not just for orphans.
A communal flat is just that—communal. Residents share
a common kitchen and a common bathroom. Many Russians pay the government to live in them because it is all
they can afford. In the early 1990s over one million of my

countrymen lived in communal flats in St. Petersburg—a city of five million. While the government is supposed to supply a communal flat to orphans, the reality is that an orphan might be on a waiting list for six or seven years to get one.

So, as my days in the orphanage system were counting down, I began to take stock of my life. If my past was frightening, my future was even scarier to me. I began, jokingly at first, to ask my American friends to sneak me home with them in their suitcase. The closer I got to graduation, the more I started to seriously pray for the Lord to make a way for me to go to the United States. I could no longer envision my life in Russia. I had no plans of how to do it, and I could not even imagine how I might get to America, but I knew somehow I would. I didn't even put myself on a waiting list for a PTU or a communal flat.

Instead, I prayed for a miracle.

11

Jesus looked at them and said, "With man this is impossible, but not with God; all things are possible with God."

—Mark 10:27

As I look back on my years in the orphanage, for as bad as they were, I can now see where the Lord placed special people in my life at just the right time. People like Melana, my original protector, Doug Jester and the Navigators, and Valentina at the police station. Some people's role was less dramatic, but equally appreciated. There was a woman named Lisa at Orphanage 51 who was a chef. We really connected. At times she almost felt like family to me. She would sneak me extra food from the kitchen. Her apartment was only five minutes from the orphanage and she sometimes invited me to her place for a meal with her son and daughter.

I didn't really see it at the time, but now I can see how much the Lord provided for me, even before I knew Him. It is amazing that in eighteen years in the orphanage I was never molested. And for all the abuse I took from older orphans and caretakers and teachers, I never even had a single broken bone.

Another one of the special people God put in my life was a woman named Joyce Bourcier. She was in Russia for two years with The Navigators. In many respects Joyce was like a mother to me for a short time. She showered me with love and care, help and patience. She gave me lots of encouragement and attention, not to mention all the hospitality she shared, opening her apartment often to me and my friends. She also played a significant role in the next turning point of my life.

There was a couple in Tucson, Arizona, in America, who had been strong supporters of The Navigators for many years. The Hugheses came to Russia in 1993 for a Navigators conference. About a year later they contacted the Navigators office inquiring if they knew of anyone from overseas who would like to come to America as a foreign exchange student. Joyce heard about their request and immediately thought of me, as I would be graduating from the orphanage soon. A lot of work had to be done, but the timing could be perfect.

My orphan status was challenging enough, but to make things more difficult, I was only seventeen at the time, a minor. Therefore I was not permitted to fly on a foreign flight without a legal guardian. Joyce began to pray about the situation. Her first thought was to act as my guardian herself but she soon realized that, as a foreigner, she could not legally take me out of the country, nor for that matter could any of the caretakers in the state system. Melana and Joyce came up with the idea that Melana would become my legal guardian. In that role, Melana could then give Joyce permission to escort me to the States. The Hugheses hired an attorney to work with the orphanage on the logistics.

I knew nothing about these plans or even the idea of me going to America as a foreign exchange student. All of this was done without a word being said to me. Joyce was rightly afraid that if things did not work out it would be a crushing blow to me.

Because she had necessarily been involved in the process, the director at Orphanage Number 51 knew long before I did that I would be going to the United States to live for a year. She also knew that I would come back to Russia, since the program was only for twelve months, and therefore she should have started the lengthy process of securing a communal flat for my return, but she did not. Instead, she closed the file on me and washed her hands of me once she learned I was going to America.

In February of 1995 I came to Joyce's apartment, the same as I had on so many other days. This time, though, Joyce greeted me with a big hug and the exclamation, "I have great news for you, Alex: You are coming to the United States of America!"

I could not contain my excitement. With tears of joy, I shouted, jumped up and down, and ran around the apartment, literally leaping for joy.

Joyce brought me down to earth with the directive, "Now you have to really study English!"

The Hugheses (the American couple who were to be my host family) paid for Joyce to arrange for a tutor, and my studies began. The next two or three weeks were extremely hard for me. I was a major pain as a student. In fact, though Christ was in my life, I still struggled with a host of sins: vanity, selfishness, stubbornness, and pride, to name but a few. I had a know-it-all attitude, and very little discipline when it came to studying. I was not used to giving my best effort on anything, much less school work. That had never been required of me.

I was an average student and that had been good enough

for me to get by. The value of education and hard work had never been instilled in me. There were days when the English lessons were so difficult I just wanted to give up. I would wail, "I don't care, I can't do this!" Joyce would respond, "You should care! This nice gentleman who is inviting you into his home in America is paying *his* money for *you* to learn English!"

Did I want to come to America? More than anything else in my life. Did I want to work this hard to get there? I wasn't so sure.

In the orphanage system the orphans graduate after the ninth grade, having received what is considered a basic high school education. On May 25, 1995, I had my last class of the ninth grade and heard my last school bell in Orphanage Number 51. By this time there were only sixteen of us left in our class, about to graduate from both school and life in the orphanage. Our official graduation would not be until June 8.

In the meantime, there was a lot I had to get done. In order to leave the country I had to show I had been accepted into an American school. Working with the Hugheses, we completed the paperwork for me to be enrolled in the Green Fields Country Day School where the Hugheses' own two boys had attended high school. Once successfully enrolled, I had to go to the American consulate in St. Petersburg with Joyce to file the application for my visa. We waited in line for four hours outside and two more hours once we got into the building. Joyce paid the application fee and I settled in for my interview.

Joyce had coached me on the interview. The American State Department is generally very concerned when they see someone with no ties back in their home country applying to come into the United States, and that certainly described me: no parents, no siblings, no aunts, no uncles, nor any other relatives. I was a red flag if ever there was one. Someone like me would be a prime candidate for illegal immigration—taking a one-year student visa to get into the country, and then disappearing.

It was important, Joyce had explained, that when I was asked if I wanted to stay in the United States, to say no, that I had no plans to stay for more than a year. All of everyone's hard work thus far could completely evaporate if I was unable to get a visa. I am sure that Joyce was praying overtime as I sat down with my questioner.

The consul who interviewed me spoke both Russian and English. Between the two languages, I completed the series of questions. She asked me things like, "Do you speak English? Why are you coming to the United States? What are you going to do with your education from America?" Sure enough, she also asked, "If given an opportunity, would you consider staying in the United States?" I assured her of my intentions to return to Russia in a year's time. She approved me for a student visa, and Joyce and I breathed a huge sigh of relief and thanked the Lord for this exciting opportunity before me.

Several days later, when I received my visa, Joyce gave me a little duffle bag. I went back to Orphanage 51 and packed up all of my earthly belongings. Never mind that I wasn't going to leave for another month—I was packed and ready to go!

On June 8, 1995, there was a graduation ceremony in the big dining room of Orphanage Number 51 for me and my fifteen classmates. All the younger orphans were at summer camp by then, so it was just us graduates, our teachers, and a few guests in attendance. Melana, our original caretaker and protector was there, of course, as was Irina, our longtime teacher. All of us dressed up for our big day. Zena, one of our teachers, and the principal presented each of us with a diploma for finishing "basic high school." We were each given a little two-page photo booklet. On one side was the student's own picture, and on the other side was a picture of the whole class. Zena also presented each of us with a little porcelain tea set.

We went around the room and each of the teachers would say something about the class. Luda, the English teacher who didn't like me (she often remonstrated me, "*You* don't speak English, *I* speak English!") gave a little speech in English which most of the kids couldn't understand; ironic, since she was the one who had supposedly taught us the language.

We had a meal together, the best meal we had ever had at Orphanage Number 51—they even served champagne. After the meal, they moved the tables out of the dining room and had "disco time," the closest thing to a "prom night" we could have.

June in Russia is called "the White Nights." Just like in Alaska and other places as far north as St. Petersburg, there are times of the year when it is dark most of the day and times when the sun never really sets. June is when the sun never really goes down; it is like dusk all night. It is a tradition during the White Nights to go boating in the middle of the night on the River Neva. For graduates it is symbolic of riding down the river to your future. The State provided boats for us orphans, and my classmates and I boated until two in the morning.

For most orphans, graduation day is the worst day of their lives because their futures are so uncertain.

But I remember graduation day very fondly. It was a wonderful day for me, and I was full of hope for the future. I was going to America. I had no idea what I would do after that, but it was exciting, and my faith in Christ was growing stronger by the day. I knew that the Lord had plans for me, I just didn't know what they were yet—and I couldn't wait to find out.

12

The fear of the Lord teaches a man wisdom, and humility comes before honor.

—Proverbs 15:33

February 3, 1995

Dear John Hughes!

Hello. My name is Alex. I'm friend of Joyce. I want some ask you. How are you? How's your life? I hope you and your family feel good. And I hope all goes well. I want tell you. Thank you so much for help. I'm very glad you like help me. What you can found for me hi school. God can be heard my pray for him. Tell me more about you and your family. Because I know just you. Joyce tell me what you have two children. If you can, give me please your pictures about you and your family. I want tell you God bless you and your family. Have my questions finish about you. Now ask question yours. What you want some know about me. Ok?

Russian people called me Alexander. I was born in 1977 year, 6 December. Now I'm 17 years and 3 months. When I was born my mom ran from me. My pape ran from me when I was born before. He is don't like children. He is just sleep with my mother and then he is gone. I don't love my mother and father. You know what? When I was baby I need in mother and father love. But nobody can gave me

93

this wonderful love. Because mother and father love just alone. What like all children who need in love. In a three year old it's my first time go to children's house. In this house was not very good.

And I don't remember nothing. I'm so sorry. And then I move another place. To another children's house N51. I move to another place when I was 9 years old. I live in this children's house N51 10 years. It's a long time. And it's this school I can live this last year. So start my new problems. Because I ran from my school. I go outside on the street to difficult hard life in St. Petersburg. I have a big problem about Army. I don't want to go to Army. If I go to Army I need go to Chechna. I think so what you know about war in Chechna. You know all people who go to war in Chechna they not back. All people died on the field. But I don't want to died. I want live long time. And now every day I go to school. In my school I study many different lessons. My school go not bad. But I don't like Algebra and Geometry. And so Geometry and Algebra go not bad too. Tell me please what you need and want from me know for hi school in America. I want tell you what I'm ready go to America to hi school. You need just tell me what I need to do. Joyce tell me what hi school go one year and then I need back to Russia. I will. I need pray for God about that. God help me and you in us plan. I hope you can understand my letter. You know just one thing I want tell you how I invited Jesus come to my life and heart. First time when I was with American people from Tennessee. They come to Russia 4 years the go. They talked about God. They sing of song and read the Bible and pray for God. I very like how they do id this. I ask some people who can help me. How God can come to my heart. And give me his holy spirit. This people they pray for me to

God and then after that my life change. God gave me his holy spirit. And I'm start read the Bible and go to church. Then I was with first comishion. Then Sam and Pam Rhine and Joyce, Bob, Rita, Rond and Kristi this last 3 teams from America with who I work and greetings. Now I'm study bible every Tuesday in evening. I study Bible with Bob and Rita Lyons. When I meeting with Joyce we just talk and pray for God and about God. Now I pray every minutes. And God help me. Because he love me and everybody on the world. I pray now too much. I pray, pray, pray for God. I'm sorry here my letter finish. God help you! God bless you! God love you!

Your best friend, Alex.

Please write me a letter. Tell me with news you have for me. I hope everything be wonderful. Good-bye! With love from Russia. See you soon. Write me a letter or some days call to Russia.

I am pleased to report my English has gotten a lot better over the last sixteen years! But even with the halting English, that letter paints a good picture of me as I was on the threshold of heading to America for the first time.

Before I left for the United States I went for a week's visit with my friends Erkki and Salme, the Finnish missionaries with whom I had stayed in touch. They sent me money for my ticket and the morning after my graduation I hopped on a bus for the ten-hour journey to Finland. I had never been outside of Russia before. The border patrol gave me a hard time because I only had a United States visa, but I made it through. Erkki and Salme did not speak Russian, and I barely spoke English, much less Finnish, but we managed to spend a delightful week together.

I was amazed when the bus crossed the border at how clean Finland was. The dark, drab colors of Russia gave way to green, mowed grass, spotless streets, and bright colors.

My next culture shock was when Salme took me to a Western grocery store for the first time. At that time there was nothing like a supermarket in Russia. It was truly amazing to see the dazzling array of food—and the quantity! And there were no lines to get in, you just entered the store when you needed to go. In Russia it was common to stand in any line you saw, even if you didn't know what it was for, because it might be something you needed.

The entire population of Finland was only as many as St. Petersburg—about five million. The town Erkki and Salme lived in was just fifty thousand people, and it seemed like all of them were tall, blond, and blue-eyed. At five-eight, dark haired, and with brown eyes, I stuck out a bit and we got plenty of second glances from people passing by.

In addition to the other differences I was noticing about life in Finland, I noted how quiet the streets were in the evening. People in Finland are very family oriented and most spend their evenings at home. I couldn't enjoy television, since it was all in Finnish, and in those days I didn't enjoy reading very much. Tomi, my hosts' son, who spoke some English, taught me to play video games, so I spent most evenings on the computer with him.

A week after I arrived they loaded me up with some food and some money and put me back on the bus to St. Petersburg. I will never forget the harsh contrast when I returned to my home country. It seemed even more drab, dark, crowded, and dirty than I remembered.

My orphanage friends Ed, Sveta, and Maria, along with Melana, all came to the airport a few days later to see me off to America. It was hard to say goodbye, especially to

Melana, but I knew that I would be back in a year's time. My departure was made easier by knowing that my friends were all in good hands. Before Melana's husband died, they lived in a communal flat. She had worked hard the past year to ensure that Edik received his own room in a communal flat upon graduation. She then exchanged her own room for one in the same building as Ed's, so they now lived in the same apartment building and she was there to feed and care for Ed (we always knew he was her favorite!). Sveta inherited a three-room apartment from her uncle who had passed away. By Russian standards she was now "wealthy." Maria received a room in a communal flat in another region of the city, but she had become friends with Nina, one of the night shift caretakers at the orphanage, and I knew that Nina was watching out for her. Nina would often have Maria over to her apartment for meals. With my friends in good hands, I was ready to see America!

I was traveling with Joyce Bourcier, who had initiated my American trip in the first place and whom Melana had signed off on as my temporary guardian, and Bob and Rita Lyon. We had to spend the night in London. I had never flown on an airplane, nor had I been to London. It was all very exciting. The Lyons were taking a different flight to America than Joyce and I, so we bid them goodbye and departed for Chicago.

We had just enough time to get through immigration services at O'Hare before we had to board another plane, this one to Tucson. In total, Joyce and I were in the air for twenty-six hours. By the time we landed in Arizona, my fascination with flying had definitely worn off.

At the airport the Hughes family were all waiting to greet us: John, his wife Thompson, and their two sons,

*Thompson and
John Hughes*

Justin and Cole. They were holding balloons and a teddy bear for me and had a sign that read,

"WELCOME TO AMERICA, ALEX!"

After John had read the letter that I had written him he thought he would need to hire a translator for me, at least for a time. On the trip home in the car from the airport I talked non-stop. John decided they didn't need a translator after all.

Eighty-five degrees is about the hottest it ever gets in St. Petersburg. My initial impression of Arizona was how hot it was—Tucson welcomed me with one hundred five degree temperatures. That first day, everything was new. I had never seen the desert, lizards, or cactus—and some of these cacti were ten-feet tall with six-inch needles. We were riding in a Chevy Suburban, by far the largest vehicle I had ever been in.

John and Thompson's house was the largest house I had ever seen. I woke up in the middle of the night that first night, freezing cold. "Where the heck is this cold air coming from?" I wondered. That, too, was a first: in my seventeen years I had never experienced air conditioning.

Even though we all knew this was a temporary arrangement for only one year, the Hugheses treated me like part of the family. It was certainly a new experience for me when John Hughes called me "son." Even more significant was the fact that Thompson Hughes gave me a kiss each night before I headed off to bed. While most American boys would be mortified to have their mother kiss them, this seventeen-year-old Russian orphan cherished the gesture, along with my new teddy bear that I slept with each night.

I found out later why they had thought to give me the teddy bear. Joyce, it seems, had written Mrs. Hughes before we left, in order to give her an idea of what she could expect having me live with her family.

> Dear Thompson,
>
> I'm sitting in a café in the most beautiful park in the world (at least that I've ever seen), Catherine's Summer Palace and gardens in Pushkin. I came just to walk around the park to just "be" with the Lord, a skill I'm trying to learn. I'm a far better "doer." Ever since I saw your family photo, I've been thinking about you and even more as the time of our meeting gets closer.
>
> As a mother, I have tried to put myself in your place. It's one thing to take an infant into your home and quite another to bring in a teenager. I have really had you on my heart all week thinking about how you must feel.
>
> The other day I wasn't feeling well and it was a holiday. Alex came over in the afternoon and watched a movie with me. He picked up my room-mate's teddy bear and sat down on the sofa. He's told me how much he really likes "toys." I think he means stuffed animals. He's not compelled to carry them around, but really likes them. It would be special if you were to shop around and find a really great teddy bear for him. This would be very special.

I've thought of how I would describe Alex to you. I've been with him quite a bit. I've seen him happy, hurt and upset. I've spoken at length to a teacher who has known him since he was a young boy. Alex is a self-conscious, sensitive young man. He has never asked me for money and has never deceived me. Now, I'm not naive and know that going to America is a high priority to him, but he's not been dishonest. I've entrusted him with money and sent him on errands. His teacher (Melana) also believes him to be responsible. He is tidy and concerned about his appearance. He is self-conscious about his teeth, but with John's skills I'm sure that will improve. Although he is 17, emotionally he is much younger.

He will need your love and understanding more than anything. I believe that God has given you those qualities. After I saw your picture, your family with my life verses on the card, I am more assured that God has chosen you to give him the nurturing he needs and you too will be blessed. He is naive in many ways but he may not show it. An example was when I took him to buy shoes. I didn't realize that he had never gone shopping for shoes. I'm sure you will be surprised by much and yet find this to be a very rewarding experience. You, John and the boys (all of them) are in my prayers. Keep your trust in the Lord and nothing will overcome you.

Both Alex and I are ready for some warmer climate. Arizona is really looking good. Today is May 16th but it is only in the 50's. Alex really loved your letter. We are both looking forward to meeting soon.

Richest Blessings and Love, Joyce
Proverbs 3:5–7

As Joyce's letter implied, I ended up in the home of an endodontist. Talk about God's perfect planning! Joyce was right: I was self-conscious about my teeth. John Hughes was shocked by the condition of my mouth, and began, almost immediately, the long process of restoration. He performed five root canals on me and then referred me to a general dentist friend of his. Prior to that, I had never even been taught how to brush or floss my teeth (in fact, I had never even heard of dental floss).

About two weeks after arriving in Arizona, John, his sons Justin and Cole, and I all flew to Seattle for a Promise Keepers men's conference. I was fascinated by the beautiful hotel we stayed in, as well as by the mass of men—some sixty thousand of them—gathered in a stadium to praise and worship the Lord. I had never been in a crowd like that.

We went to an upscale Italian restaurant for dinner on the first night and I was amazed at the menu with its pages and pages of choices. I had been to a few restaurants in Russia with my Navigator friends, but in the Russian restaurants the menus were single pages with just two or three choices.

My American hosts' sense of humor, and especially their sarcasm, was new to me. Justin and Cole told me that it was the custom to pay for your meal by offering to wash dishes. Taking them at their word, I rolled up my sleeves and told the waiter that I was ready to hit the sinks. I was so mad when I found out the boys were kidding me that I didn't speak to them for the rest of the night and refused to sleep in the same room with them. My "brothers" still ended up having the last laugh, as getting any actual sleep in their father's room proved impossible. I had never heard a grown man's snoring before, and it kept me up all night!

Tucson and Seattle were not the only places I visited that summer. I had tried my best to keep up with the dozens of missionaries I had met over the past few years in St. Petersburg. (I should point out that many of the people I call "missionaries" were not full-time missionaries but lay people who had volunteered to do short-term missions projects in Russia.) Two of them, Scott and Carol Perry, lived in Connecticut and they invited me to visit them there. Scott commuted to New York City every day and he took me into the city for a wonderful day of sightseeing. But the most unusual experience on that trip was back in Connecticut.

One day I went with Carol to a Bible study and met a woman named Patti. At church that Sunday I saw Patti again and met her two daughters. Patti invited me over for lunch. Beyond the gated drive was Patti's home, a mansion, unlike anything I had ever seen. We had a nice visit and while I was there I met Patti's husband, an unusual looking man named Keith.

When Carol came to pick me up after lunch, she asked, "Do you have any idea who you just had lunch with?"

"Yes," I said. "Keith and Patti Richards." That's when Carol explained to me that Patti had been a super model and Keith was *the* Keith Richards, of Rolling Stones fame.

Later that summer I had the opportunity to go for a week to the Navigators' summer camp for high school kids in Colorado Springs at Eagle Lake. I am sorry to say that I was not at my best on that trip. We hiked about fifteen miles a day and I became known as the whiner and complainer. I complained about the heat, the heavy pack, my sore feet, and the (in my mind) purposelessness of the endless walking. I was a city boy, and this walking around with forty pounds on your back was crazy to me.

It's pretty funny, as I look back on it, considering all I had been through—including walking much further distances in much worse weather—that I would be the one to complain.

At the end of our time on the trail we did something called a "solo." Each of us kids had to take our own pack into the woods by ourselves and camp overnight, spending twelve hours alone with the Lord. I was not at all excited about this. I didn't like the idea of being out in the bear-laden woods alone for the night. I was comforted that I was only about two hundred yards from the camp, and I could see the campfire in the distance.

Not very interested in the exercise, I promptly set up my little camp and went to bed. Because I had turned in so early, I awoke before the sun arose the next morning. I watched it rise over the Rocky Mountains and was moved by the splendor. For two hours I prayed, read Scripture, and sang. It turned out to be a wonderful experience, one that my know-it-all attitude almost spoiled. By the end of the camp, despite all of my grumbling and complaining, I had to admit to the group that the trip had been great. In retrospect I hope my whiny attitude did not hurt the other kids' enjoyment of it.

Thanks to Americans I had met in Russia, my summer tour of their amazing country continued. I was able to visit friends in California, where for the first time I had the opportunity to share my life story with a gathering held for that purpose. I sensed right away that there was something very different in their reaction than in that of Russians. Russians, especially during the Soviet time, all had their own struggles, and as a result, most of them had little time or sympathy for someone else's struggle. There was a sort of life-is-tough-get-over-it attitude from most.

I was very moved by this experience of telling my life story to a room full of compassionate American Christians.

America was fascinating to me, from the profound (the response to my story) to the mundane (twenty-four hour forecasting on the Weather Channel—I could watch it for days!). Seeing the ocean for the first time and the power and miracle of creation in the crashing waves before me was another profound experience. Long, hot showers and shopping malls were other American habits I quickly became used to.

Alas, summer came to an end, and Green Fields Country Day School started classes toward the end of August. I was excited, but apprehensive to begin school. Green Fields had about two hundred students and I would be enrolled in the twelfth grade. It was one thing to speak English well enough to communicate, it was something else altogether to think about taking all of my courses in the language and having to both speak and write in it.

School started out difficultly. I made friends easily enough, and the school's small size was a help, but classwork was hard. Some of the processes were so different from what I had learned in Russia—problem-solving in math, for instance—that I found myself having to unlearn some things in order to re-learn them. It was frustrating. The language barrier proved to be bigger than I thought, too. While I could speak English fairly well by then, composition was all new to me. This grammar and punctuation stuff was like a whole new foreign language to me! I barely made C's that first trimester. The Hugheses were kind enough to hire a tutor, and by my second trimester my grades had improved, to mostly B-pluses.

The Hugheses never treated me as a guest. I truly felt like a member of the family. They even introduced me to friends as their "Russian son." John insisted on giving me an allowance, which I refused at first. I didn't need the money, all of my needs were being met. But then John explained that it could be my spending money and that it would be good for me to begin to learn to manage money. Instead, I learned to save money, stashing much of it away. (Later, when John found out that I had been saving much of the money, he was impressed and matched, dollar for dollar, the $200 I had socked away.)

John was becoming increasingly frustrated with my academic efforts, or lack thereof. When checking my homework one night, he was appalled that I would settle for doing every other math problem, for instance, even though that was all the assignment called for. Since I had trouble in math, he thought I should want to do *all* the problems just for the additional practice.

While John's insistence that I strive for excellence was annoying to me, he was doing it out of love. No one had ever challenged me to that standard and the idea of striving to be successful was new to me. But excellence was not my goal in life; survival was. Russian orphans don't tend to have long-term goals, rarely looking beyond the next meal, and in my mind, I was doing great.

Unfortunately, we both dug in our heels and a tension and frustration ensued between us. We were talking over each other, it seemed, and I was not able to accurately convey my gratitude for all they were doing for me.

In December of that year John made a decision. He pulled me from Green Fields and enrolled me in the University of Arizona at Tucson in the English as a Second Language (ESL) program. It was an intensive English program that would prepare me for the Test of English as a Foreign Language (TOEFL). A passing grade on the TOEFL was required of any foreign student applying for admission to an American college or university, which was what John wanted for me. He even offered to pay for me to go to a four-year college if I passed the TOEFL. College was John's way of motivating me. For my part, I just wanted to stay in America; if college would do that for me, then college sounded great.

I graduated from the ESL program in May 1996. I then took the TOEFL. I needed five hundred fifty points to pass it. I came up fifty points short the first time I took the test and forty points short when I took it a second time a week later (grammar was my downfall).

If I was disappointed, John was "done." He thought I must not be very serious about the opportunity he was offering; at the very least I must not be ready for college. He was extremely disappointed and shared with me that he was finished trying to motivate me.

"I can either send you back early to Russia, or you can work at the Navigators' camp all summer."

Despite whatever misgivings I may have had about working at the camp all summer, the alternative was much worse, so I headed back to Eagle Lake.

There were hundreds of kids at camp, and a large number of staff. My bunkmate was a guy named Danny. I worked in the kitchen and Danny was one of the counselors. Each night when we went to bed, Danny stayed awake with his flashlight and Bible, reviewing his memory verses. He often asked me to quiz him and I was fascinated by his ability to memorize Scripture, something I had never attempted to do.

When Danny noticed my interest, he offered to help me do it myself. I told him I wanted to memorize 1 Corinthians 13, "the love chapter." I memorized a few verses every day and before the week was up, I had all thirteen

verses memorized. Danny and I developed a deep friendship over that summer, studying and committing God's
Word to our hearts.

By now summer was over, and so was my time in America. I had arrived in the United States with only a small
duffle bag and now I was leaving with a large suitcase, two
big boxes full of belongings, the allowance money I had
saved, and deep friendships across the continent. But I
had no idea where my belongings or I would go once I arrived back in Russia.

13

*May he give you the desire of your heart and make
all your plans succeed.*

—*Psalm 20:4*

I got back to Russia in September 1996. I had no job, no
education, no place to live, and only four hundred dollars to my name. I had no plans for my future, just a dream
of living in America. Most importantly, though, I had my
faith in God. I thanked Him time and time again for all
His blessings.

My year in the United States had been incredible. I had
seen more of the country in one year than many Americans do in a lifetime. I had been to the Atlantic Ocean and
walked along the Pacific coast. I had travelled to California, Washington, Indiana, Connecticut, Colorado, and
New York. I had cooked and served meals to hundreds of
people each day at the Navigators camp, experienced life
with a healthy family, and even been to a rock star's home.
I was sorely disappointed to be back in Russia, but my survival mode kicked in. I would figure something out, and I
would have to trust the Lord for His plan for my future.

For those first weeks back I stayed at various places,
with American and Russian friends. I survived mostly on
bread and tea. I did some tour guiding and translating,
making just enough money to get by—barely.

Later that fall, Sue Gregg came back to Russia for about

a month to do more cooking seminars and she stayed with our mutual friends, Mel and Mary Lou Duke, who headed up the Navigator work in St. Pete.

The Dukes suggested that Sue hire me as her "gofer," tour guide, and translator. It was wonderful to be back with Americans again. When Mary Lou had to fly back to the States because her father was ill, Mel did not think it looked right for Sue to be staying at his apartment with his wife gone, so he invited me to move in with them. Now I not only had a really nice apartment but I also had meals for the first time since being back in Russia. After Sue left to go back to California I stayed at the apartment with Mel. I continued to be amazed by the Lord's blessings in my life.

When Mel had to go back to the U.S. in December he asked me if I would be willing to stay at the apartment while he was gone. Would I ever! I was thrilled. I might have been back to surviving mostly on bread and tea again, but at least I enjoyed them in nice surroundings.

In addition to my American Navigator friends, I also spent time with my old friends Misha and Marina (the former ballerina and her husband who took me in for several months the final time I ran away), and of course, Melana. And I was more determined and focused than ever on studying my English.

One day Mel notified me that Sue had enjoyed working with me when she was in Russia and that she and her husband Rich wanted to invite me to come to California to live with them for a while, where Sue would train me in cooking.

Truth be told, I had absolutely no desire to learn to cook, but I welcomed another opportunity from the Lord to get to America. I began the arduous process, once again, of obtaining a visa.

At Rich and Sue's suggestion, I applied first for a three-year business visa at the U.S. consulate. That request was denied. Then I thought I might improve my chances by asking for a six-month visa. It turned out that changing my request from a three-year visa to one for just six months was just a big red flag to the American authorities. With absolutely nothing holding me to Russia—no family, no job, and no home of my own—I was seen as an illegal immigration risk.

After the second rejection, a very kind gentleman who worked at the consulate pulled me aside. "You seem like a nice young man, Alex, and pretty determined. But you don't have enough evidence for why you are going to America." He then gave me a list of supporting documents I should provide to help make my case. He told me he would personally review my request when I came back.

Each time I applied it meant filing another $100 fee (a fortune for me), filling out more paperwork, and waiting in line for hours. Each time, my prayer efforts increased. I just knew that God wanted me to go back to America.

I went back for the third time, this time with a stack of documents, including a paper I had written and letters from the Dukes and the Greggs, just as Richard, the consular official, had suggested. After again waiting in line for several hours, I realized that he was not at the consulate that day. Yet, after waiting so long, and thinking the extra documents would help, I went ahead and applied again, this time for a three-month visa.

The response came quickly: application denied. I ran out of the consulate in tears.

Some Navigator friends who had been helping me with my paperwork, Bob and Suzanne Achgill, called Richard at the consulate as soon as I told them my news. He apologized that he had not been there when I came in. "Tell him to come back tomorrow," he said, "and I will personally review his request."

True to his word, Richard was there the next day. At the close of the interview he had just one question for me, "Alex, will you come back?"

"I give you my word, I will come back."

I left the consulate with a six-month visa in hand.

The process of getting the coveted visa had taken three months, during which I continued to study my English. It paid off. In February of 1997 I took the Test of English as a Foreign Language (TOEFL) once more, and this time I passed with flying colors.

Having passed the TOEFL and gotten my visa, it was time to celebrate. I invited Maria (my old classmate who was to have been adopted with me when we were younger), Ed, Sveta, and Kostya over for dinner at Mel's apartment (Kostya's mother was our orphanage director so he was in Orphanage 51 all the time and for a while attended school with us). We all had a nice dinner and cake to mark the occasion and then took a ride downtown. Melana had gotten a car for Ed so that he could work as a driver, which he had been doing for some time.

It angered me that even though he was making money as a driver, Ed never gave any money to Melana and he never even offered to pay her back for the car. What I was seeing in my friend was something I saw in lots of orphans—a "you owe me" mentality that creeps in after years of everything being provided for you by the State. Looking back, I wish I had been as quick to see that fault in myself as I was in others. It would have saved me from learning the lesson the hard way later.

Even though I didn't appreciate Edik's lack of gratitude

toward Melana, I nonetheless enjoyed having a friend with "wheels." It was an unusually warm evening for early March in St. Pete so we got ice cream and wandered around downtown until 2:00 in the morning. I had to get up at 4:00 to catch my early flight. That morning, March 11, 1997, my friends took me to the airport. Just six months after arriving back in Russia, I was once again on a plane heading for America.

*Off to America again! Me, Kostya, Melana, our friend Valya,
Sveta, and Edik at the airport to see me off*

14

Be joyful in hope, patient in affliction, faithful in prayer.

—Romans 12:12

When I entered the United States for the second time, this time arriving in Los Angeles, my visa was stamped "NO EXTENSION OF THE VISA. MUST LEAVE COUNTRY IN SIX MONTHS." No explanation was given why this rather unique stamp was put on my 1-94 card, but it was clear that my visit had a strict limit this time.

Sue and Rich Gregg had a cookbook company, Sue Gregg Cookbooks ("Whole Foods for the Whole Family") and I was put to work right away. Sue felt like cooking would be a good vocation for me, and one of the purposes for my visit was to learn that trade. I also helped Rich with the business side of things. "Help" might not be the right word. At nineteen, I had no real interest in math, accounting, or, frankly, the cookbook business. We clashed, due in no small part to my immaturity.

I felt rather locked in a prison. I had no friends in California, no car or transportation, and the Greggs seldom went out. It was "all work and no play." While they did take me to Disneyland and Sea World, it was not enough to satisfy my insatiable appetite for exploration and socialization. The best part of my time there was the time that Sue spent with me every morning studying God's Word and praying for the day.

It was decided that a change was desirable, so Rich offered my catering services to many of their church friends. I enjoyed the social aspect of meeting folks and serving at dinner parties, but, as anyone in the catering business can tell you, the hours of preparation were grueling. Some of the families even took me in for a day or two to stay in their homes in preparation for their parties.

Emotionally, I was struggling. "Lord," I would pray, "is this what you have planned for my life, to be a cook?" I have the utmost respect for people who serve the Lord in occupations like food service, but this did not feel right for me. I loved America and did not want to leave to go back to Russia, and that time was quickly approaching, but I had no real passion for cooking and the entire experience had been difficult for both the Greggs and me. I missed spending time with friends and desperately wanted to see God's plan for me and for my future.

One particular day, when I was at an especially low point emotionally, I wrote Rich and Sue a letter telling them that I was not going back to Russia, but I was moving on, nonetheless. I knew that going back to Russia meant more suffering, and in my almost twenty years, I had suffered enough. I figured that with my increasing grasp of the English language and my "street smarts" I could find my way in America.

I packed all of my stuff in a suitcase and kept it hidden under the bed, with the letter, waiting for the opportunity to run away. I had no idea where I would go or what I would do. No plan. I just knew I didn't want to go to Russia, and I didn't want to stay on with the Greggs.

One day shortly after I tucked the suitcase and letter under my bed, Sue and I were at dinner at a restaurant in a nearby town. We talked about my chef training and our conversation turned into an argument. I lashed out at her, "Leave me here. I'll walk home later!"

With that, I got up and ran out, leaving Sue at the table crying. I hid in the bushes, waiting for her to leave before I started walking. I was still very stubborn—and still very lost.

I walked along the freeway berm, crying, praying, and contemplating as I walked. I felt like I couldn't take any more of the ups and downs. At times I felt so blessed and so close to God. Other times I felt incredibly depressed and lonely.

Over the roar of the traffic, I shouted, "God, what do You want me to do? You've given me so much, but I have no idea what to do. You have a plan and a future for me. Lord, what is it?" Just as soon as I began shouting questions to the Lord, a cloud cover came across the sky and, just as suddenly, I had complete peace. I didn't have any answers, but the peace was a welcome relief.

I walked for hours, and when I finally returned to the Greggs' house I apologized to them and confessed that I had been planning to run away.

Shortly after that night, I knew in my heart that I was supposed to go back to Russia. Yet I still had a strong urge to go to college in the United States, so I went to a local college to get information. A school official took one look at the special stamp on my visa and knew she needed to call an immigration attorney. The attorney informed her that there was absolutely no way to change that six-month work visa into a student visa. I was devastated by the finality, the lack of freedom to do what I wanted to do. Yet, despite the disappointment, it confirmed for me that, regardless of my own desires, God wanted me to go back to Russia for the time being.

Despite whatever temporary difficulties we had during my stay there, I had grown very close to the Greggs, particularly Sue. I was like a sponge around her; she showered me with so much attention, care, and motherly love. She gave me assurance and strength and helped fill an empty spot in my life.

In 1998, when she was on another mission trip to Russia, Sue offered to adopt me. Not legally, of course, but she wanted to fulfill the role of a mother in my life. I agreed, and over the years, the bond has continued to grow stronger. Rich, too, has played an important role in my life and his support of me and my ministry have been a tremendous blessing.

Rich and Sue had three children, two girls and a boy. Not long before I was born, when he was only three years old, their son Steven had been killed by a drunk driver. Many years later, when Sue was in her forties, a woman told her she would have another son. Sue did not put much stock in this "prophecy." The woman repeated her claim some months later, getting a similar response from Sue. Yet it was not long after this that the Lord prompted Sue to "adopt" me. Maybe there was something to this prophecy, after all. The Greggs have now been married for almost fifty years. What a privilege it has been for me to be a part of their family and their family gatherings over these last thirteen years.

Before I left, Sue hosted a surprise dinner party at the church as a going away event for me. During my time there I had served meals for dozens of different families and many of them came to say goodbye. Sue made a scrapbook for me of photos from my time with them. They also presented me with numerous gifts of cooking supplies: a skillet, knives, a cutting board, a tablecloth with matching napkins and napkin rings, measuring cups, cooking spoons, and a chef's hat and apron. Sue also gave me a certificate of completion for chef training.

Cooking supplies in hand, I boarded another plane and headed back to St. Petersburg, still no closer to understanding what I was to do with my life.

15

I am not saying this because I am in need, for I have learned to be content whatever the circumstances. I know what it is to be in need, and I know what it is to have plenty. I have learned the secret of being content in any and every situation, whether well fed or hungry, whether living in plenty or in want.

—Philippians 4:11–12

Once again, I was "home" in Russia with all of my earthly possessions. They were still confined to a few boxes and a large suitcase, but were far more than I had ever owned. Unfortunately, I had no home to go to.

Ed and our friend Kostya met me at the airport. While it was great to see my buddies again, it was depressing to be back in Russia, especially with no plans for my future. I hated being there. As much as I felt I was where I was supposed to be, I had no idea why, and my heart still longed to be in the United States.

The first few weeks I moved around a lot, staying a night here and there with friends. Not wanting to overstay my welcome, I moved often. I ended up finding a spare room with a man named Boris, a Russian friend of Mel and Mary Lou Duke. For $75 a month, I had a place to call home. My finances were helped by $20 each month that Sue Gregg was sending me out of the goodness of her heart.

Boris' place was my first experience living in a communal apartment. Sharing a kitchen and a bath with strangers was a little disconcerting to me. I never disclosed to my fellow tenants that I was an orphan, or even that I was Russian. I spoke English well enough by now that folks assumed I was an American student in Russia (ironic, since what I wanted to be was a Russian student in America!). I did nothing to correct their assumptions. I knew that my new community would look upon me differently if they knew I was actually a Russian orphan who had been homeless before I took the extra room in Boris' flat. I hated it there but tried not to complain. It was God's provision for me and it surely beat the streets. Taking my cue from Matthew 6:34—"Do not worry about tomorrow, for tomorrow will worry about itself"—I tried to take one day at a time. As Jesus said, "Each day has enough trouble of its own." I felt certain that the Lord would soon reveal to me His plans for my future. But had I known that I would live in this communal apartment for the next four long years, I probably would never have agreed to the arrangement.

The bathroom stunk worse than an outhouse. I had to hold my nose every time I used it. The floor in the bathroom was old and wooden and was rotted all around the toilet and the tub. The whole toilet would wobble and rock and the tub had no shower curtain. I suggested that we all put in a little money together and buy one. Their reply was unanimous: "You want one, *you* buy it."

I made a trip to the store and bought air freshener, toilet paper (we each had to bring our own every time we went to the bathroom), scouring powder, and a shower curtain. I had to string the curtain up with rope, but after a while they all loved the new addition. It took me over an hour of scrubbing out the tub to get it acceptably clean.

It looked like it hadn't been scrubbed since the Stalin era. Regardless of my continued efforts to keep the bathroom clean, my fellow tenants often complained that I was in the bathroom too long.

The $20 a month from Sue was a help, plus I got a few odd jobs here and there as a tour guide or translator. But while I could always count on the $75 rent being due at the same time each month, I never knew when my next job was going to come. I lived mostly on bread and hot water. (As I explained to my friends, hot water was just like a cup of tea—only without the tea!)

While I was able to improve the bathroom a little, there was another problem in the communal apartment that proved more difficult. The apartment was on top of a small grocery store. Next door to them was a produce market. Convenient, yes, but St. Petersburg is known for its rats, mice, and cockroaches, and living near all that food made it worse. As soon as the lights were turned off at night, hoards of cockroaches would rush in. If you happened into a room at night and turned on the light, you would see an army of them scurrying across the floor and dropping from the ceiling.

One evening when I decided to splurge on a meal, I turned on the stove and hundreds of roaches ran out of it. I decided then and there that I would never again cook in that apartment. So much for chef school.

In addition to the varmints, there were the vagrants, the homeless folks who "took up house" in our enclosed stairway, sometimes defecating, oftentimes vomiting, on our stairs.

Obviously I never felt comfortable inviting guests over to the place. Ed and Sveta each came once or twice, and Mel and Mary Lou Duke came one time. For four years those were all the visitors I had. The Hugheses, my host family in Arizona, had given me a little boom-box and it became my sole source of entertainment. I spent hours listening to Christian music.

In my heart I knew that this was a testing time for me and the experience deeply humbled me. It made me appreciate all the more my time in the States, and even my years in the orphanage. I knew that the apartment was better than the streets but I also knew that I wanted better for my life.

During this time I occasionally visited Orphanage Number 51. I spent time with the kids and visited the caretakers that I liked. I also looked for every opportunity I could think of to get back to America. It was almost all-consuming for me. That probably hindered me from bettering my life in Russia—whenever I felt I couldn't take my life in the filthy apartment any longer, I stayed on a little longer because I just knew that God was going to open another door for me to go back to the U.S.

My desire bordered on desperation, and I paid a price for it. One day as I was walking downtown I saw a billboard that said, "If you want to become a student in America, we'll help you." I found the company and excitedly walked into their office. The lady shared with me about a student program for a school in New York to study English. I took most of the rest of my savings and paid the required fees. Over the next few months I spent a good deal of my time filling out papers and more papers. Supposedly, I was repeatedly denied by the American school. This did not make sense to me, and I was crushed to find out that the entire thing had been a scam. There was no student program and no school in New York looking for foreign students to study English.

The director of this agency was a woman named Natasha. She had noticed my determination and approached me to help her begin a legitimate immigration company to help Russians get to other countries. She would give me a job in the new company, but she needed some money to help start the new venture. I would be paid well for my work and they would pay back the loan as the company grew. Best of all, the new company would help me get back to America. I took what remained of my savings and gave it to her.

Natasha started the new company. We had a nice office in downtown St. Pete. I served as a consultant for the agency and helped folks complete the necessary paperwork to get their visas for America. I was paid for the first two months. It was an exciting time for me: I worked in a nice office doing important work, I made good money, and soon I would be able to return to the United States. Life was good. Then, after the first couple of months, Natasha stopped paying me and the company's other employee. She assured us that it was only temporary, that once the company began making more money she would give us our back pay.

Before long I began to notice that, while I wasn't being paid, Natasha was living very well. I also found out that she had stolen $5,000 from a former business partner. I realized that I would never get my back pay and I would never see the money I had loaned her. I had fallen for her scam not once but twice. I felt like a fool; and now, a very poor fool.

I survived by being a facilitator for various ministries and made a modest income, just enough for meals. I also began to go to Orphanage Number 51 on my own in a more official capacity, to teach cooking, English, Bible studies, and organize birthday parties. All the while, I continued to put in a few hours each week at Natasha's company, trying to maintain a relationship with her, hoping to find out what she was really up to. I also thought that if she was a friend she would feel obligated to pay me my money. However, the longer I was there, the clearer it became that I would never see my money. It didn't help that I was afraid of her husband, a former policeman. I didn't know what to do. Once again, though, the Lord provided a protector for me, the same one He had used in my life so often before.

I went to Melana and poured out the whole story and admitted how foolish I had been. She went the next day and confronted Natasha and her husband. He immediately began to threaten Melana that he would involve the police. Melana did not back down. She had her own connections with the police, she explained, the SWAT team in particular.

"If I have to come back, I'll bring the SWAT team with me!" she shouted.

The next day I got back the money I had loaned Natasha.

I never did get my lost wages, but I didn't care. It was a tough lesson, and I just wanted to put it behind me.

Once a week I would do my laundry at Aunt Marina and Uncle Misha's house. It was also a social event: We would have dinner together and watch television or play games while my clothes were washing. They had an old Soviet-era washing machine with no spin cycle and they did not have a dryer. I had to wring everything out by hand. I would then put it all in a big plastic bag and lug it back to my apartment, a half-hour's walk away. I would hang it all up from a rope tied up in my room and wait, sometimes for days, for the clothes to dry.

A recent picture of Tetya Marina and Dyadya Misha

It was an inconvenience, yes, but those inconveniences and living conditions were beginning to make me very appreciative. After years in the orphanage system, I realized that I too had developed that entitlement mentality that I found so unattractive in my friends. It was a slow, painful, process, but I could feel the Lord chiseling away at my imperfections. For probably the first time in my life, I was learning to be content in my circumstances and, moreover, to be grateful and appreciative for what I did have. What Paul wrote in Philippians 4 was becoming true for me: "I have learned to be content whatever the circumstances. I know what it is to be in need, and I know what it is to have plenty. I have learned the secret of being content in any and every situation, whether well fed or hungry, whether living in plenty or in want."

16

Praise be to the God and Father of our Lord Jesus Christ, the Father of compassion and the God of all comfort, who comforts us in all our troubles, so that we can comfort those in any trouble with the comfort we ourselves have received from God.
　　　　　　　　　　　—2 Corinthians 1:3–4

I was in Russia this time for four years. Though I was learning to be content with my circumstances—little money, little food, no regular job, and a less-than-desirable place to call home—there was one thing that I really struggled with: I had no idea what my future held.

I could not get a good job because I had no education. In Russia, without a college degree there is little hope for a decent job. And even that didn't help sometimes. At that time, there were people with master's degrees working in the new St. Petersburg McDonald's.

Even more than my lack of education, I did not seek a permanent job or any kind of future plans because deep in my heart I was still determined to return to America. The sporadic work that I did have was the result of the many friends the Lord had put in my path over the last several years, mostly Americans. They came back to Russia from time to time or had friends and friends of friends who came. I was a valuable resource as a tour guide and translator, enough so to maintain my lifestyle, which was not much more than a roof over my head with bread and water.

Even though I didn't have a plan, God did, and He was working during those "wilderness years" to shape my heart and mind toward His things.

I had been visiting Orphanage Number 51 for some time and had taken on more of an official role, teaching English and cooking, and leading Bible studies with some of the kids. The more I was there, the more I began to realize their needs. The government supplies were inadequate. Each child, for example, got only two pairs of socks and underwear per year. Toilet paper and toiletries were scarce.

I expressed my concerns to several of my American and Finnish friends and they began to send me money to buy supplies for Orphanage 51. I would go all over St. Pete to find good deals or companies willing to give me discounts on, say, three hundred pairs of underwear. I would take pictures of all the supplies I bought, attach the receipt to the picture, and send them to the friends who sent the money. I wanted to not only show that I was grateful for their generosity, but accountable for every dollar they sent.

Before long, this work became like a full-time occupation for me. It also became my passion.

There are about one hundred and twenty orphanages in St. Petersburg and its suburbs, housing about ten thousand orphans. I felt the Lord calling me to expand my efforts beyond Orphanage Number 51, and began calling some of the other orphanage directors. In doing so, I truthfully said that I was representing various individuals who wanted to help. I would never identify myself as an orphan, however, or even as a Russian, feeling my work would lack credibility to them because of the stigma in Russia regarding orphans. These directors heard my by-now fluent English and saw me so often with Americans that I imagine most of them assumed I was an American. I did nothing to dispel the notion.

I visited forty orphanages and ended up working with twenty-seven of them. As my own experience showed, there are three levels of orphanages in Russia: the baby level for newborns to four-year-olds; the kindergarten for five- to seven-year-olds; and those like Orphanage Number 51, for seven- to seventeen-year-olds. The needs at the baby orphanages were vastly different from those like Number 51, and the needs at each individual orphanage were unique.

Mostly I bought medicine, diapers, and clothing for the baby orphanages. For those in the third age level, in addition to underwear and clothing, I sometimes bought furniture and washers and dryers.

The number of people giving to my efforts grew as I shared the need with more of my foreign friends. God was answering my prayers in a mighty way and it was always a joy to see how and when the funding would come in. The contributors were a combination of different individuals as well as organizations, all scattered over several countries. Their only connection to each other was me, and a shared desire to serve the Lord by serving the orphans.

Proverbs 16:9 says, "In his heart a man plans his course, but the Lord determines his steps." This was certainly the case with me. I had no grand plan—certainly no "business plan"—no formal structure, nor did I have any intention to build an organization or career for myself. Yet God was putting together a system to provide for the needs of orphans in St. Petersburg, and using me to do it. Along the way, He allowed me to develop quite a reputation at many of the orphanages, most of whom still had no idea that I too was a Russian orphan, now emancipated and living in squalor with very little income of my own.

Sadly, many Americans made promises to me that they did not keep. It was a tough lesson but the Lord used it to teach me to never give promises that I couldn't keep. When the orphans asked me for things, I never promised I could get them; I simply said that I would try.

I also knew firsthand the corruption in the orphanages and had watched too many times the goods intended for the orphans being carried out by workers. I made it my personal policy to deliver the goods and gifts directly into the hands of the orphans themselves. Knowing, too, that orphans are not all angels, I sometimes had to put conditions on the gifts. One summer, about fifty of the kids from Orphanage 51 were going to summer camp. Most of them had no tennis shoes, and those who did had shoes with gaping holes or tape holding the soles in place. They begged me to bring them tennis shoes for camp. I told them I would try, but I sat them down and told them that if any child sold the shoes to buy alcohol or cigarettes I would no longer bring any more gifts to Orphanage 51.

I asked Edik to go with me to shop for the tennis shoes. Ed was ashamed of his past and wanted nothing to do with orphans and never told anyone he was an orphan. I wanted to give him the opportunity to experience the joy I felt in helping the kids. I didn't know it at the time, because I didn't understand it myself, but looking back I realize that I also wanted to share with him the healing process that I was beginning to experience. I often talked to Ed about God and he had attended church and Bible studies sometimes with me, but he never really discussed spiritual things and, to my knowledge, never made a commitment to Christ. Ed reluctantly agreed to shop for the shoes. When we took them to the camp and delivered them into the hands of the kids, the kids were of course thrilled. Even better than that, for me, was to see how Ed was touched by the children's response.

Later that summer, I went back to the camp with my dear friend Sherry Oxendine. She and her husband were some of the first Americans I ever knew and had talked about adopting me for a time. Sherry brought along an illusionist who used magic tricks to talk about God. While at camp I learned that the older kids had sold their tennis shoes and had a beer party. That did it. I told them that I was done helping Orphanage Number 51. The younger children came to me and begged me not to. Some of them had had their shoes stolen by the older kids, but they had surely not sold their shoes. It was very hard for me, but I stuck to my word. I still helped Orphanage 51, but no longer at the individual level. In the future I bought some couches and some dressers and continued to supply toilet paper, but I no longer delivered gifts into the hands of the orphans there.

All of this was a learn-as-you-go proposition. Shortly after I supplied couches for a couple of the floors at Number 51, kids and caretakers alike began grumbling and complaining because they did not get new couches on their floors. Their ingratitude hurt me deeply and I was tempted to walk away. I prayed for the grace and strength to press on.

Not long after that the director at Orphanage 51 asked me for help on a big project of replacing all the pipes and redoing all the bathrooms in the home. It was a huge project, by far the biggest I had taken on. In addition to keeping up the communication and accounting (sending receipts) to the donors, I also had to keep the funds coming in and line up the contractors and contract the work as the funds were available. All along the way I continued to get nasty comments and snide remarks from caretakers and kids. Lyudmilla, my old English teacher, took every opportunity to make nasty comments to me. It was very difficult and frustrating work, as well as a thankless job. Upon the completion of the project I had been assisting Orphanage 51 for almost two years and I was done. It was not so much the lack of appreciation for my efforts as it was a change in my heart and direction from the Lord.

For all the hours I spent on the plumbing project and for all the satisfaction I felt when it was finished, I began to realize that big projects for the whole orphanage had little or no direct impact into the lives of any orphans. I realized that I was not interested in just supplementing the needs of the orphanages, filling the gaps left by the government. All of this had started because I felt a tug in my heart to minister to orphans. It took me two years of focusing on quantity to get to the desire for quality. No longer was I just interested in buying three hundred pairs of underwear or a truckload of diapers. I needed to connect with a few individuals and really make a difference in their lives.

The Lord began to lay on my heart individual orphans in whom I saw great potential. I knew that I needed somehow to focus on their inner healing and their need for Jesus. As usual, I didn't know where this was all heading, and I started small. I spent the next two years with this individualized ministry focus at Orphanage 51, while I continued to help the other homes with large quantities of goods. I wanted to duplicate in others the life-changing effect the Navigators had on me. One of their key verses is 2 Timothy 2:2. "And the things you have heard me say in the presence of many witnesses entrust to reliable men who will also be qualified to teach others." That's what I increasingly wanted to do. I was no longer "chasing the numbers."

I tried to find time and resources to also spend special time with kids in the other orphanages. I knew that I couldn't impact the individual lives of all the orphans I met, but I needed to do more than just supply them with goods. I have always loved children and it broke my heart to visit Baby Orphanage Number 8 where most of the babies laid crying in cribs and most of the kids were crowded in a playroom, crying to be picked up and held. Sometimes I would just go spend time holding and playing with the children. When God provided the means I would take them to the circus or McDonald's or the park.

After years of watching me, one of the directors came to me one day and asked, "Alex, why do you do what you do?"

I knew that it was time to share the truth with someone. I told her the short version of my life story. She cried and cried and hugged me. She told me she was sorry I was raised in Orphanage Number 51, which did not have a good reputation in the system, and that she was amazed that I had turned out the way I had. She had even more respect for me now in my work with orphans.

I never set out to form an official ministry or a designated organization of donors to meet the needs in Russian orphanages, and I was certainly not intent on building a career for myself in Russia. I was simply an emancipated orphan myself with a lot of free time on my hands who was learning to listen to the still, small voice that was directing my steps and softening my heart. The words of Paul in Second Corinthians were taking on new meaning for me: "Praise be to the God and Father of our Lord Jesus Christ, the Father of compassion and the God of all comfort, who comforts us in all our troubles, so that we can comfort those in any trouble with the comfort we ourselves have received from God."

17

*He who is kind to the poor lends to the Lord, and
he will reward him for what he has done.*
                                    —*Proverbs 19:17*

The International church I had attended with my Navigator friends closed. Once the foreign missionaries left and a Russian pastor took over, attendance dwindled to almost nothing, so it was disbanded. Through an English-language newspaper that I treated myself to once a week, I found a new church home in St. Petersburg.

At church I met a visiting group of missionaries. They hired me as a translator and I took them on a tour of Baby Orphanage Number 8. One little boy's story broke my heart. Misha's mother, a prostitute, had turned him over to the orphanage so that she could live the good life in Italy with one of her wealthy clients. Hearing a story of a mother discarding her child like that hit me hard. I broke down and cried for this little boy I didn't even know. It brought back all sort of issues I had concerning my own mother. Through those tears I realized for the first time that my work with the orphanages and my passion for the orphans were the beginning of my own inner healing process. Something I wrote around that time helps explain the feelings I was having:

Often in my life I ask the Lord to comfort my heart and give me peace regarding my biological mom. I pray to be healed of bitterness, regardless of the pain that abandonment has caused me. I try to imagine what it would be like to meet her after all these years. Over the years I have begun to have a measure of peace that I so desperately pray for. I try to imagine her circumstances, her fears and inadequacies that led her to discard me. I try at some level to have compassion for her, but the anger and the hurt and the devastation take aim at any ounce of compassion I can muster. One thing I do know, however: If it were not for her, I would never have been born to be so blessed by God.

At that time, Melana happened to be with children at the Sunnyville sanatorium. I felt the need to go see her as I struggled through my feelings. As always, she was a great comfort to me. She provided a shoulder for me to cry on and always understood me. Sunnyville was a long way from both the city and the orphanage and they sometimes had a difficult time getting supplies. I committed to helping them, along with the other orphanages with whom I was working.

On the train ride from Sunnyville back to St. Pete, I suddenly got the urge to visit my once-adoptive parents, Kolya and Larisa. To this day I don't know why I went there. I had no idea what I would say and no preconceived notion of my own expectations. I got to their home only to find out from the neighbors that Kolya had gotten a promotion and they had moved closer to the city to a nicer home with running water. The neighbor gave me their new address. I went to the new home and rang the bell, still not knowing what I would say if they answered.

Beloved Melana

As it turned out, they were very friendly and welcomed me in, inviting me to stay for dinner. Our conversation was very superficial. We never discussed the past at all. Over the coming weeks as I continued to make the train ride to Sunnyville I often stopped to see them. I think I visited another eight times or so over the next many months. As with that first reunion, we never discussed the past; there were no apologies, no explanations, no repentance. When I tried to talk to them about the Lord, they had no real interest.

Even though I didn't quite understand at the time why I kept going to visit them, I knew somehow it was important to my healing process. Somehow it was necessary in order for me to be able to move on with my future. In fact, the more I ministered to individual orphans during this time, the more compelled I felt to go visit Kolya and Larisa. After a while, I realized the lesson the Lord was teaching me. I couldn't just talk to the orphans about love and forgiveness, I had to live it. My walk needed to match my talk. Those little orphans had incredible instincts. They knew when you meant what you said. They knew genuine.

There is a verse in Ephesians 4 which says, "Get rid of

all bitterness, rage and anger, brawling and slander, along with every form of malice." I needed those visits in order to do just that and to forgive these people who had abused me and destroyed my hope. It didn't matter that they acted like nothing had happened. It didn't matter that they didn't offer explanation or apology. It only mattered that I was able to forgive them. Thanks to the grace of God, and the love that He continued to pour into my life and His abundant forgiveness of me, I was able gradually to do so.

I continued my work with individual orphans and also did some work with the Texas-based Buckner International, one of the largest adoption ministries in the world. I met some wonderful folks from Buckner and have continued to keep in touch with them.

Sarah and Christian were two of those folks. They had decided to adopt two Russian brothers, Dennis, eleven, and Dima, ten. After their first efforts were unsuccessful, they asked for my help. I had absolutely no experience in foreign adoptions but I was excited to dive in for the sake of those two boys. It proved to be a valuable learning experience. I spent hours learning the ropes, hunting down documents, delivering documents, and filing documents.

When I finally delivered the case to the court the judge asked, "Who is the facilitator for this case?"

Not knowing what else to say, I declared that I was the facilitator. That made my role official and I was even given the power of attorney from Sarah and Christian.

Regardless of the country, adoptions are difficult and a labyrinth of paperwork, meetings, and waiting. Russia is no different. Unlike many in my country, however, I was not willing to pay any bribes to expedite things. I chose instead to stay on top of things and follow up frequently. In the case of Dennis and Dima it took about four months to get our court hearing. It was my first appearance in an adoption hearing. Since both boys were over the age of ten, they had to appear at the hearing to give their consent to be adopted. The adoption was complete, but I had little time to reflect on the accomplishment or to relish the joy I felt in seeing this family united. They were off to the American Embassy in Moscow to get physicals for the boys. I dashed off with the court documents to get them translated and would meet up with the new family in Moscow (since I was not a legally certified translator I could not do the job myself).

This was just the first of many times that I had the privilege of helping folks facilitate the adoption of Russian children in the years ahead. Russia no longer allows independent facilitators; today one must work through an approved adoption agency. But there is so much corruption and red tape and delay in the process that I am still asked to help from time to time. Christian and Sarah continued to grow their family. They adopted two more Russian orphans, Victor, age seventeen, and Anastasia, age fourteen. They have also had two biological babies.

I kept up my efforts to return to America during this time. I unsuccessfully applied for the U.S. green card lottery three years in a row, after which I gave up. Regardless, I still felt strongly that I would be returning to America one day. I continued to pray for that opportunity as I lived day-to-day in Russia, making the most of every opportunity the Lord brought my way and seeing His hand in my life every day.

Often opportunities would arise for me to take individuals on a tour of St. Pete. For example, an American family came to St. Petersburg from Moscow for two days. To conclude our tour I took them to Orphanage 51. It was their first time to visit a Russian orphanage and they were very moved and made a generous donation to the physical needs of the boys there.

It was opportunities like these that the Lord brought my way that sustained me in those years. They were my only source of income. It was wonderful to see how the Lord tied those work opportunities to my ministry. It was a constant reminder to me that He is continually at work in my life and is using me to touch the lives of others.

18

Forget the former things, do not dwell on the past.

See, I am doing a new thing! Now it springs up; do you not perceive it? I am making a way in the desert and streams in the wasteland.

—Isaiah 43:18–19

My friend Mel Duke received his next missionary assignment from The Navigators and was now preparing to move to Estonia. Mel and Mary Lou needed my help with the move as all of their boxes were in the communal apartment where I was living. I went through the process of getting an Estonian visa since I was going along in the truck to help unload and, more importantly, to help out at the border with the customs agents.

Mary Lou went on ahead of us on the train and would meet up with us in Estonia. I purchased her train ticket for her and sent my suitcase on with her because there was not much room in the truck.

The night that Mary Lou was scheduled to leave on the 8:00 train, I was babysitting for some friends. As I was washing the dishes I heard a clear voice say to me, "Call Mary Lou." Three times I heard it and three times I ignored it. I could not imagine why I should call her or what I would say when I did.

Later that evening, long after Mary Lou had departed,

With Mary Lou and Mel Duke

and after the kids I was babysitting were in bed, I was writing emails. Suddenly, it hit me: my passport and visa were in the suitcase on the train with Mary Lou!

I was thrown into a panic. As soon as Bob and Suzanne (the parents of the children I was babysitting) returned, Bob and I jumped in his car and headed to the train station. We stood in line and explained what had happened.

Normally, the Russian response would have been unsympathetic. "Tough luck. Next customer!" Surprisingly, and no doubt due to Bob and Suzanne's fervent prayers on my behalf, the ticket agent we spoke with was determined to help.

"Do you know what compartment and what seat Mrs. Duke has on the train?" she asked.

Fortunately, because I had bought the ticket for her, I had that information and reported it to the ticket agent.

Looking at the timetable she saw that there was one more stop for the train, in a city twenty minutes before the Estonia border. The police in that town were called and they agreed to locate Mary Lou when the train pulled into their city.

I spent the night at Bob and Suzanne's, having been told by the agent to call her back the first thing in the morning to confirm that they had retrieved my documents.

Nervous and anxious, I prayed that the Lord would take care of the situation. Once again, the Lord answered my prayer. I felt a peace come over me, and I actually enjoyed a great night's sleep. I called the ticket agent at the earliest possible moment in the morning and confirmed that the police had retrieved my passport and visa from Mary Lou. My documents would be waiting for me when Mel and I drove there on our way to Estonia. We retrieved them without incident.

The border crossing, however, was not nearly as smooth. It took almost three hours on the Russian side and an additional hour in Estonia. The border agents went through all of the sealed documents and belongings to attest to all of the belongings in the truck. Once we made it through all of that, we still faced three more hours of driving as the rain turned to sleet. We even had a flat tire to top it all off.

Mary Lou was relieved when we showed up, a few hours late and the answer to lots of prayers. I stayed with the Dukes for four or five days, helping them unpack and settle in. I was going to miss them a lot. They had become like American grandparents to me. But the Lord was about to put yet another amazing American couple in my life.

Mark and Melinda Cathey had served as missionaries in St. Petersburg since 1992. They worked with a group called Church Resource Ministries (CRM), helping plant and develop churches in the former Soviet Union. I met them through some of my Navigator friends sometime in 1996. It was just a casual meeting, but I took note, as I always did, of the foreign Christians I met along the way.

It wasn't long after my Estonian experience that I showed up at the Catheys' doorstep, ringing their doorbell and hoping they would remember me. I love the way that Melinda tells the story. In the years since, I have heard her tell it many times.

> I can still remember that first time Alex came to our door. It was November and freezing cold and there he was in just a white t-shirt. He must have pegged us as "rich Americans." He was offering his service as a "personal chef." With a house strewn with toddlers' toys and screaming kids, I don't know if I said it, or just thought it, but a personal chef was the last thing I needed!
>
> But just as I turned him away with a "Thanks, but no thanks," to his offer, I was immediately hit with a Bible verse. It had been a long time since I heard or read this verse, yet it came to mind, word for word: "This is how we know what love is: Jesus Christ laid down his life for us. And we ought to lay down our lives for our brothers. If anyone has material possessions and sees his brother in need but has no pity on him, how can the love of God be in him? Dear children, let us not love with words or tongue but with actions and in truth." (1 John 3:16–18)
>
> It literally scared me when that verse came to mind. Not only was it clearly from the Lord, but because I had no means or need for a personal chef, I had just turned away a lonely, hungry orphan who didn't even have a coat. The Lord would not release that verse from my heart or Alex from my thoughts. I knew I must make contact with this young man.
>
> That encounter with Alex, and then the Lord speaking to me through that encounter, was life changing.

Hers was not the only life that changed as a result of that cold November encounter, nor was mine. It would set into motion events that finally revealed to me God's calling on my life, and as a result of that calling, bring into being a ministry that God continues to use to bless the lives of Russian orphans.

A few days after I showed up at their door the Catheys invited me over for a meal, to get to know me. They began to introduce me to their Church Resource Ministries friends and show me their exciting work. We hit it off. In many ways, the Catheys "adopted" me like a brother, even including me in their family Christmas celebration. They had a nice washer and dryer and allowed me to come and do my laundry at their home. When my passport expired they gave me the money to renew it. They fed me well and frequently and even gave me chicken and beef as a Christmas gift. I was welcomed into their home and felt very much a part of their family. When they left for vacations, they would ask me to stay at their apartment which, given my own communal living situation, was like a wonderful vacation for me.

As she got to know me and more of my life story, it stirred something in Melinda's heart of compassion that led her, a busy missionary and mother of three, to want to accompany me to the orphanages to see what she could do to help. I certainly did not expect this of her, considering all of her other obligations and duties. It was just something that the Lord put on her heart.

Since they had lived in Russia for eight years, the Catheys had a car. That made visiting the orphanages much easier. Soon after that first dinner, Melinda began traveling to orphanages with me once or twice a week. Together, we started working with about fifteen different orphanages.

This was in addition to another twelve or so that my work with Buckner International, my friends Sherry Oxendine and Lena Engel, and my summer camp work put me in touch with.

The more we visited the orphanages, the more Melinda became aware of the inadequacies of the Russian orphanage system. She got an in-depth picture of how poorly the system prepared these kids for their emancipation at age seventeen or eighteen.

Often when we left an orphanage, Melinda and I would sit in the car and cry and pray. She saw firsthand that the government system was designed to meet the basic physical needs of food, clothing, and shelter, but the children lacked any personal care, affection, guidance, or preparation for the future. It was through our talks and prayer sessions in the car that our ministry was birthed.

Like me, Melinda saw that since the fall of communism, missionary dollars were flowing into the orphanages, yet it did not change the outlook for the orphans' futures to have nicer bathrooms or hot water. There was still no real investment in their morality, their spirituality, their identity, value, dignity, or purpose. We watched, over time, as orphans left the system, hopeless. In fact, the Russian society honestly believed it would be better for everyone if they just died.

After one of our trips, Melinda and I were sitting in the car, praying. She began to get angry with God and cried out, "Where are You, Lord? Why don't You *do* something?" Just as clearly as she had heard the passage from First John when I showed up at her doorstep, she immediately heard a quiet voice say, "Why don't *you* do something?" It changed her perspective from one of anger and frustration to one of determination.

"Alex," she said, "this just can't go on! We aren't making a dent in their lives! What can we do?" she asked.

I suggested a program for the graduates. Then the brainstorming began. "What does that look like?" she wanted to know.

I answered from my heart and my experience: what I had, what I didn't have, and what I needed. I thought back on what had helped me the most and what had made a difference in my life. The most significant of those things were my faith, the exposure I had received to Americans, to other Christians, and more importantly, to people who cared.

I remember telling her, "Too many missionaries believe you just bring the gospel and lead people to the Lord and then they'll be fine. Yet, that is just the starting point. You need to deal with the emotional baggage of these orphans, working through attitude and emotional changes, forgiveness, and validating these kids as individuals."

The key to all of this in my own life had been accepting Christ as my Savior. But, "If you want to break the cycle of hopelessness, crime, prostitution, and drug abuse," I told her, "these kids need someone to journey with them and love them as they set off on their new journey."

We carried on this conversation over the course of an entire year. Melinda was very thoughtful in her questions, and I brought the perspective of having walked in the shoes of the people we wanted to help. "What do they really need to prepare them for life outside the orphanage?" she would ask. It was through these tears and talks, and probings and prayers, that our vision for a program for graduated orphans was birthed.

Together, we identified the crucial aspects of our program that would help them become productive members of society. Without a doubt it would need to be a hands-on, family-based, residential program.

We decided to share our idea with a few of the orphanage directors we had worked with to gauge their response. By then, Melinda had seen what I had long observed: Russians do not exhibit compassion. They have no tolerance for listening to someone's troubles because everyone has troubles. Also, none of the directors we surveyed knew that I was a Russian orphan. Lastly, most orphanage workers were there simply for the pay. They had no heart for orphans and no interest in investing in their lives. We were pleasantly surprised, then, that many of the directors were verbally supportive of our vision, at least initially.

Yet, at some level they all questioned, "Why would you do this? What's in it for you? Why go to all this trouble, when these orphans are destined to die on the streets?"

This was nothing new to me, but it was an eye-opener for Melinda. When she realized just how careless the society was with its orphans it made her even more driven to see our vision through to reality.

Orphanage Number 46 was one of the largest homes in the system and it was the only one we found that shared any of our passion for emancipated orphans. Lubov, the director, actually fought for the rights of orphans. Orphanage 46 consisted of three buildings, only two of which were used for the orphans' residence and school. The third building had been turned into a vocational school and a small housing section for emancipated orphans. We were thrilled with this discovery and eagerly attempted to team up with Lubov because of her passion and persistence.

When we shared our vision with her, she introduced us to her assistants and even let us interview some of the emancipated orphans and some of her soon-to-be-emancipated orphans to better understand their needs.

After a promising start, our cooperative efforts hit a brick wall when Lubov learned that our vision was just that: a vision. We were not an accredited program with the Russian government.

"Then I can't give you any of my children," she snapped. Our discussions ended.

It is important to remember that even though orphans in Russia graduate from the orphanages at age seventeen or eighteen, they are still wards of the State until age twenty-three. The orphanage director is technically the legal guardian for all the emancipated orphans from her orphanage until that time.

The more Melinda was exposed to the system, the more determined she became—and the more frustrated. There is a vast difference between what's in "the book" and what happens in real life. In the Family Code of the Russian Constitution there is a whole section on "The Rights of Orphans," including the rights of emancipated orphans. It is this section of the Constitution that we orphans refer to as "the book."

According to "the book," emancipated orphans have the right to higher education, paid for by the State. In reality, however, the vast majority of orphans are never accepted, primarily because they are not academically prepared.

There are two hundred thousand orphans in Russia in the state orphanage system. Ninety percent of them are "social orphans" and once emancipated are required to go back to live with their relative or family, back to the same situation they were once taken away from, mostly to one-room communal flats. Rather than live with an abusive, alcoholic, or incompetent relative, most of them choose to stay with their fellow orphans, sometimes six or seven to a room. They basically join the ranks of street children, except they sometimes have a room in which to sleep.

The ten percent of orphans who are "true orphans" are, by "the book," supposed to be given a room in a communal apartment, yet there are far more orphans waiting in line for an apartment than there are apartments. To buy some time, the government will send true orphans to a trade school with a dormitory until a room opens in one of the communal flats. Yet, the government decides which trade school, and the dormitory living conditions are far bleaker than the orphanages from which they came.

Melinda saw for herself the run-down Soviet-era dorms, complete with their missing windows, leaking roofs, lack of hot water, and broken beds. She talked with orphans and most were thinking, "What's the point in going to trade school when society won't hire orphans, anyway?"

For the few who do attend trade school, the government pays them a monthly stipend of about $75; but orphans who have never had money don't understand the value of it and have no experience managing it. It is not uncommon for an orphan to spend $100 on a pair of Levi's or to spend their whole monthly allotment on drugs or alcohol or cigarettes and then have nothing left to live on for the rest of the month.

In addition to the financial woes, Melinda was seeing that the concept of education and learning escapes these orphans. They are generally two grade levels below their peers at these trade schools. If an orphan in elementary school doesn't understand the lessons there is no one "at home" to help them. Most of them give up.

For all these reasons, along with the emotional issues of hopelessness, isolation, and depression, the vast majority of emancipated orphans begin to make poor choices, choosing the streets as their "home" and selling drugs and their bodies, or stealing, to survive. At least ten percent of them end up committing suicide.

Almost fifteen thousand orphans are emancipated annually in Russia. Within the first five years, ninety percent of them end up in the world of crime, homelessness, and drugs. Those are bleak statistics, disturbing to most who hear them. To me, and increasingly to Melinda, these were not statistics. These were my friends. They were names and faces. We were not disturbed, we were frantic. We were frantic to end the cycle, to somehow make a difference.

19

So do not fear, for I am with you; do not be dismayed, for I am your God. I will strengthen you and help you; I will uphold you with my righteous right hand.

—Isaiah 41:10

Melinda Cathey and I had no idea how to go about getting licensed in Russia, nor did we have any idea where we would get the money to support our efforts. Yet we believed strongly that our vision was from the Lord and that He would guide our steps.

As we prayed and thought through the ideal ministry to emancipated orphans, we determined:

• The program must be a residential program.

• It has to be a family environment.

• It must address emotional needs, not just the physical needs. We had to address the participants' dignity, self-worth, purpose, motivation, and direction.

• The orphan's spirituality was key. We both knew that I would not be where I was without my faith in Jesus. Faith in other people or the government had always failed me. It had only been as I grew in my faith in God that I was able to begin to hope and change. We knew we needed to not only share the good news of salvation with the participants but also help them grow in their faith.

• The program must address basic life skills. In the

orphanages everything is done for the orphans. They never learn to cook, clean, pay bills, sew on a button, or balance a checkbook. They certainly never learn—or even need—to find a job.

• Orphans in Russia don't get a full high school education. A successful program would have to address that. Additionally, we knew we wanted to motivate and prepare them for higher education and careers.

• For some, higher education may not be an option. They have talent, but it needs to be validated and they need to be given opportunities to use those God-given talents. To survive and become self-supporting contributors to society, they must have the opportunity to learn vocational skills.

As we continued our work with the orphanages, while laying out our vision for this new work with emancipated graduates, we were led to a ministry to street children in St. Petersburg called Project Life. Though run by Russians, it was supported by the American ministry, Voice of the Children. Licensed in Russia, Project Life offered a shelter for some twenty-five or thirty street children, ages eight to seventeen. Project Life had rented the fourth floor in a dormitory building but were only using half of it.

The director was a woman named Lena, and Melinda and I were excited as we realized that she and Project Life were real answers to our prayers about how to get started. She offered to rent out the other half of the fourth floor dormitory to us. Equally significant, we were offered the opportunity to come under the legal umbrella of Project Life; therefore, the time, money, and red tape involved in becoming a licensed agency in Russia could be delayed.

Further, it gave us a vehicle through which we could begin to raise funds. Donations to our "Project Life II" ministry could come in as tax-deductible gifts through the Voice of the Children ministry.

Lena even asked if we would be willing to take two of her girls from the shelter. Since the girls were eighteen, they were technically too old for Lena's program, but she did not want to put them out on the street. At the same time, the Lord led us to two other girls living on the streets of St. Petersburg, whom we interviewed and accepted into our fledgling program. Thus, our new ministry began with four residents, in one-half of a fourth floor dormitory, next to a homeless shelter for kids, and under the legal umbrella of the Project Life/Voice of the Children ministry.

With our vision rather suddenly and remarkably becoming a reality, Melinda and I were now faced with new challenges and opportunities. One day Melinda asked me, "Alex, what would you like to do for Project Life?"

My answer was immediate. "I would like to go back to America and raise funds for this project."

Melinda was ready for that. "Okay, first I want you to contact any Americans you know and share with them our vision and why you'd like to come to America and see if they support the vision. See if they will let you speak at their churches and home groups."

She didn't need to ask me twice. Soon, the emails were flying from St. Pete to California, Texas, New York, Arizona, and every other state where I had made friends over the years. I had nine years of relationships to build upon. Within two weeks of my first email I had lined up close to one hundred and fifty events that would take me to sixteen different states in the U.S.

We immediately began the paperwork to get a visa for me. Melinda went with me to the American consulate where we waited in line over five hours. The Lord was clearly blessing these efforts as I was quickly granted a three-month business tour visa for the purpose of fundraising for our Project Life ministry.

It was June 2001. I was twenty-three years old and, after a four year absence, I was headed back to the United States. Only this time, I had more than just my own future in mind!

20

*In everything I did, I showed you that by this kind
of hard work we must help the weak, remembering
the words the Lord Jesus himself said: "It is more
blessed to give than to receive."*

—Acts 20:35

The next three months in America were a whirlwind
of different cities, airports, host families, new friends,
and reacquainting myself with old friends. I was on an airplane every week. I met people in their homes and in their
churches. The fellowship was sweet, the warm welcomes
were encouraging, and the sense of belonging and purpose were exhilarating.

I didn't know it at the time, but I was stepping into my
calling and feeling a peace I had never experienced. More
than just sharing my passion for the new ministry and
seeking support, I was opening up and sharing my own
life story with total strangers and feeling empowered and
blessed in the process.

The support I received was not always monetary.
Through connections I made on the trip I met a man
named Adam at a large Russian Evangelical church in Atlanta. He said, "I don't have any money to give you, but I
can design and maintain a website for the ministry." He
created a wonderful site for us, free of charge, a real blessing. Still more people offered to pray for us on a regular basis. I felt those prayers as I travelled around the country.

Initially, I assumed that "the bigger the better," when it came to speaking to churches. I figured the more people I could see and speak to at one time, the better the chances of gaining supporters. Yet, the Lord showed me early on in that trip that the possibility of personal connections and commitments was much stronger in smaller groups. When I spoke at large churches my allocated time and my ability to connect with individuals were very limited. The most I could hope for in those situations was a "love offering." While I was appreciative of every dollar given, the Lord taught me that what I was really to be seeking in America were partners, people who would support us with both their prayers and their financial generosity. In fact, many of the original donors from that trip in 2001 continue to support our ministry today.

One large congregation I spoke to was a Russian Slavic church in Atlanta, with about twenty-five hundred members. Though by that time I had learned that bigger was not always better, I still welcomed the opportunity to connect with my fellow countrymen in America. Of course I knew that most Russians don't want to hear your troubles and that, in general, they are a very unsympathetic group. In fact, that's ultimately the reason why I was traveling the States fundraising, rather than Russia. So, I approached the opportunity with very low expectations. You could say that I had more curiosity than conviction about this particular engagement.

I was amazed by the responsiveness of the people.

Many approached me after the service who were caring, supportive, and generous. It was as though the Lord was showing me that being in the United States had softened these Russians' hearts. They were able to see beyond their own pain and their pasts. They had been absorbed into the society of very charitable Americans and that exposure had literally changed their Russian culture to one of generosity. I was astounded when the gathering produced a love offering for the ministry of over $5,000.

Their open hearts were a testimony to me of the power of God to change lives. The whole trip was an affirmation to me that what Melinda Cathey and I were doing was truly God's ministry and that God would provide.

Back in Russia, Melinda was continuing to move forward on faith. She knew we needed to find a pastor to help with the spiritual direction of the ministry, and that we would need to find workers. Here, Melinda's husband Mark proved to be a real blessing to us. The ministry he worked for, Church Resource Ministries, specializes in training and developing Christian leaders. One of the men Mark was mentoring was a Russian pastor named Pavel, a graduate of St. Petersburg Christian University. In exchange for Mark's continued mentoring, Pavel agreed to serve as the pastor for our work, free of charge.

Pavel had a lot of connections with the Christian university and he suggested Melinda meet with Ira, Luba, and Katya, all graduates of the school.

Luba admits that at the time she had no desire or calling to work with "the least of these." With her multiple degrees (in Theology, Management, and Counseling), she was looking to start a career, not for opportunities to volunteer. Yet, when Luba met Melinda she was very moved by her story. She was touched by Melinda's passion and vision and stepped out on faith to accept what was then the unpaid position as director of the ministry.

Katya, likewise, felt led to donate her time as our Christian counselor, and Ira, as our first mentor for the emancipated orphans in the program.

So, as I was journeying through the heartland of the United States and the Lord was touching the hearts of many Americans, back in St. Petersburg the vision was taking root, and God was bringing together the hearts and hands that would translate our vision into reality.

If it was up to me, I would have stayed longer in the U.S. But my visa was set to expire on September 15. As with every other opportunity that had brought me to the States, the days for this trip were numbered. I was set to fly from Atlanta to Chicago, from where I would fly on to Russia.

My flight to Chicago was scheduled for Tuesday morning, September 11, 2001.

It gave me a sense of solidarity with my dear American friends to be in my adopted country, in an airport of all places, about to board a flight, on the morning of that fateful day.

Of course all air traffic was halted when the terrorist attacks happened that morning. Not knowing how long the airports would remain closed, I immediately called the immigration services to ask what I should do; my visa would run out in only four days. They had no answer for me, nor any interest in my affection for America or my American friends, and simply stated, "You are required by law to leave the country."

In a real answer to prayer, the airports resumed flights on September 14. I was able to catch a flight to Russia just before midnight—literally minutes before my legal status in America would have expired.

The flight back to Russia was an emotional time for me. Being in the States on 9/11 in many ways made me feel even more tied to America. I was as shocked and pained by the events of that day as Americans were. I was also sad to be leaving America again. On the flight home I reflected on the places I had been and the people I had met. I didn't know if I would ever see any of them again.

I also had no way of knowing if my trip had been successful in meeting the objectives of raising money to start our ministry. I felt that I had successfully delivered the message and I knew that people were touched. But I also knew there were many worthy ministries out there. "Project Life II," as we were calling our venture, was just one more, and a small, unknown, untested one at that.

As I was praying about all of this and reflecting on it, unbeknownst to me, the money was beginning to come in. It seems that, while Melinda, Luba, and Katya were transplanting the vision into reality back home, and I was sowing seeds in America, the Lord was watering. I had no idea how much money in total I had raised, nor did I have any idea whether the ministry would really come together or not.

When I landed in St. Pete, I found the ministry already in operation. On September 3 the doors had been officially opened to the four girls. Fully staffed with volunteers, it was a real step of faith for all, with no income or money in the bank.

That was not the only surprise I received when I got back. Soon, we heard from the Voice of the Children ministry, the organization under which, through their Project Life outreach, we were raising funds. "You need to find someone else to handle your donations," they said. "We just can't handle it." It seems that the pledges from the American trip were flowing in, and had overwhelmed their ability to process them. All told, the trip had generated $126,000 in donations.

God was doing something miraculous indeed.

21

Therefore, my dear brothers, stand firm. Let nothing move you. Always give yourselves fully to the work of the Lord, because you know that your labor in the Lord is not in vain.

—1 Corinthians 15:58

While I may have been back "home" in Russia, I was still without a home, so my first order of business was to find a place to stay. Once again, the Lord provided.

Christian and Sarah were the American missionaries whom I met back in 1999 and helped to adopt their sons, Dennis and Dima. Since that time, they were back and forth between the States and Russia with their ministry work and they maintained an apartment in Russia. As it turned out, as I was returning to St. Petersburg, they were leaving to go back to America. I moved into their apartment and split the rent with them, a situation which helped both of us.

The next twelve months were all about the development of the ministry. It was the closest thing to a full-time job I had ever had. Though no longer in America, I spent a good deal of my time staying in touch with all of our donors and updating them on the progress of the ministry.

Our next priority was to replace Voice of the Children as our non-profit administrator. We landed on the organization Mark Cathey worked for, Church Resource

Ministries (CRM). Saying goodbye to VOTC was difficult, especially for Melinda. She could see their heart for children and she was blessed by their ministry, thoroughly enjoying our brief partnership. VOTC worked with younger children and it was Melinda's hope to offer "both sides of the coin," with our focus on the older, emancipated orphans. But not only could that small ministry not handle our administrative needs, the differences in focus of the two ministries became more and more apparent.

Finally, it was a Russian lawyer who told Melinda, "You can't do what you want to do with VOTC. There are different laws with younger kids and different rules for their short-term, crisis intervention. You need to focus on your program and your identity and the laws that you need to follow."

Much of the year was focused on training Luba to be the director: how to work with the Ministry of Education, the Ministry of Social Welfare, the orphanage directors, and how to select orphans for our program. Out of the thousands of orphans who graduate out of the system every year, only about ten percent have any motivation or desire to become productive citizens. Therefore, we needed to be selective in who we took into our fledgling program.

We realized that we needed to be recognized by the city authorities and get licensed if we were to work with orphanages and get the kids right when they graduated. I set up a meeting with a woman named Dina at the Committee of Education. I knew her from back in my Orphanage 51 days when I used to run papers to her from our orphanage's director.

Six years after I last saw her, I walked into Dina's office with Luba. I was now twenty-four years old and Dina did not recognize me at first. I was a little disappointed at that, but then, as she began to remember me, she was pleased to see that I was doing so well.

When we shared our vision of our ministry with her, she pointed to a file cabinet overflowing with folders and said, "I've got plenty of those programs. I don't need one more!"

Yet I knew there was no other private, non-government organization working with orphan graduates. Because it was such a novel concept it was hard for her to grasp the vision. By the end of our conversation she said she wanted to come to see what we were actually doing before she would give her recommendation to the Ministry of Justice, where we would ultimately have to go to get approved and licensed.

Dina did come to Project Life II, numerous times. She was pleasantly surprised and very positive. Her only concern was that we were so small and could only handle a few orphans. She was concerned that we would only chase "the best of the best" and wondered, "What about all the rest?"

As we began the process of filing for licensing we moved out of the Project Life building that we had rented from VOTC and found our own apartment. Thus, there was no longer any connection with VOTC or Project Life. If we were going to go through the difficult process of getting licensed we needed to come up with our own name, as "Project Life II" no longer made sense. We now had a new apartment (a miracle in itself) and now, as the next step in our growth as a ministry, we needed a new name.

Melinda and I started writing down potential names. We narrowed it down to twenty different ones. Melinda liked the name The Harbor. St. Petersburg is a harbor city, and she liked the image of a harbor—a safe place, a place of refuge. My English dictionary told me that "harbor" can mean several things: a place on the coast where vessels may find shelter and protection from rough waters; a place of refuge; or, as a verb, to give a home or shelter to. All of those perfectly matched what we were trying to do.

But the word and the image were American. Melinda needed to make sure the word would work in Russian. We showed the entire list of possible names, in her language, to Luba. Without knowing our preference, she immediately landed on *pristan* ("harbor" in Russian) and said, "This is it!" Luba explained that *pristan* was both a beautiful and a very evocative word. We knew we had found our mark.

Luba went to the Department of Justice and began the onerous process of filing The Harbor with the government. It took months, but in 2003 we became "official." After years of heartache and prayers, envisioning and pleading, over the plight of the orphans, the Lord affirmed our efforts to *do* something.

For Melinda it was born out of her gift of mercy and her heart of love and compassion, as well as a strong admonition from the Lord. She likened it to childbirth—a painful process, a lot of work and anguish along the way in parenting, but a joy that surpasses it all. For Luba it was passion fulfilled. With her qualifications, she could work any number of other jobs with fewer hours, better pay, and less heartache. But she was called to The Harbor by her passion for this life-changing work. For me it was all of that: love and compassion and passion; a calling from the Lord to *do* something. More than that, though, it was a purpose. The work of The Harbor brought purpose to my life.

22

But I trust in you, O Lord;
I say, "You are my God."
—Psalm 31:14

The Lord was busy molding and shaping me. Sometimes that process was downright painful. I remember going to Melinda one time expressing my concern that some of my American friends were not responding to my letters. I felt that they had cut me off. I was feeling rejected and didn't understand why. Melinda suggested that I speak to her husband Mark. Apparently, Mark had been waiting for just the right to time to approach me, and I had just handed him the opportunity.

He directed me to sit down and instructed me to listen, not talk, and to not be defensive. He proceeded to describe my snobby, arrogant, know-it-all attitude that may have worked for me in my survival mode growing up, but did nothing to serve me in my efforts now for the Lord's work.

It was very hurtful to hear, but I also realized that it was difficult for Mark to tell me these things I needed to hear. I had to receive it and process it quietly. This was one of my first, but certainly not my last, lessons in humility.

As 2001 had turned into 2002, Mark and Melinda had begun to be concerned about their own children. They were getting older now, and there were no good missionary school options for high school. The Catheys had been in Russia for ten years at that point and were beginning to feel it might be time to leave Russia and head back to the States. They began to pray about it and pursue career options if they did leave the mission field.

Around this same time one of our donors agreed, at Melinda's suggestion, to allow his gift to be used to pay for an American college education for me. I could hardly believe my ears. Was my dream going to come true?

I think I looked at every college in America, or at least it felt that way. After I had gone to the websites for about a hundred different schools, Melinda suggested that I narrow it down to the Columbus, Ohio, area. Her brother Chuck was active in a large church there and she thought that would help me find a good housing situation. Franklin University, in Columbus, soon became my best option. It offered the same tuition regardless of your home residence, so there were no out-of-state (or in my case, out-of-country) fees; the school thus attracted a large number of foreign students. They also offered both a two-year associate's degree and a four-year bachelor's degree. I was thrilled when Franklin accepted me as a student in the associate's degree program, to begin in January 2003.

Mark was able to find a different position within CRM back in the States, so in June 2002 the Catheys packed their household and headed to Minneapolis. Our work, at this point in time, was not even a year old. Losing Melinda's guiding hand in St. Petersburg would be tough on everyone. With my plans to leave by the end of that year, both co-founders would be gone. Even though Melinda would continue to be involved long-distance, the staff began to freak out a bit. They all knew the Lord had blessed the ministry, but they seemed to be shaken by the loss of the co-founders. "Where do we go from here?" they wanted to know. None of us were sure, we just knew that all of this was from the Lord.

During 2002 I continued to work odd jobs, mostly as a translator, tour guide, and errand boy for missionaries. The Harbor gave me purpose, but not a paycheck. During one of those errands I met a woman with the unusual name of Punkin Durio. As was my habit when meeting new American friends, we exchanged contact information. Punkin was planning a return visit to St. Pete in a year or so and I was more than happy to help make arrangements for her. Meeting Punkin would turn out to be one of those chance encounters that was not a chance encounter.

Punkin, I discovered, was a real missionary hero. She was in Russia heading up a group that was touring the country showing the *Jesus* film (a ministry of Campus Crusade for Christ). This single mother of two grown boys did such work for eleven years, traveling to some of the most dangerous places on earth so that people could hear—and see—the story of Christ.

In June 2003, she returned to Russia as promised. I was back in St. Pete for the summer and I accompanied her and her twenty-person team for several days as we presented the *Jesus* film to refugee camps, orphanages, and other places.

At the end of that trip, Punkin had everyone write notes of encouragement to the other members of the team. She really struggled with what to write to me. She kept getting the sense that the Lord wanted her to offer to be a mother to me. She decided to sleep on it.

When she woke up, Punkin was even more certain that the Lord wanted her to offer to be a second mother to me (Sue Gregg being the first), so she wrote the letter.

We were both surprised when we exchanged our notes that morning, as my note to her was very similar to the one she had written me. We both agreed that the Lord wanted us to have this special relationship.

The Lord has a wonderful sense of balance and completion. In my life I have had two mothers abandon me: my birth mother and my adoptive mother. Now, as of that morning in June 2003, He had seen fit to give me two new mothers, Sue and Punkin, who have both been true to their promise to always be there for me.

23

A generous man will prosper; he who refreshes others will himself be refreshed.

—Proverbs 11:25

In November 2002 I was headed back once again to the U.S.A. I celebrated Thanksgiving with Melinda's family at her brother Chuck's house in Columbus, Ohio, and I was about to get a chance to meet the family and see the place I would call home for the next few years.

I had heard a little bit from the Catheys about the family that had agreed to take me in, but I didn't know what to expect. I did know, though, that with every family I had stayed for any length of time, I had experienced some level of problems. I knew from my instruction from Mark that I needed to humble myself, but I was still struggling to learn how. I had grown up with no experience of living in a family. From my limited experience living with American families, I knew that Americans have high expectations, but I also knew they didn't always share those expectations with me; it was my responsibility to figure them out and then to meet them. I was not fearful of the family, the Davises, but I entered this new family opportunity with some level of concern that this would be just one more demonstration of my inability to meet expectations.

College, on the other hand, was a different matter. Of that I was very fearful! It had been almost seven years since

I had done any school work. To say I was apprehensive is putting it mildly.

I met the Davises on Thanksgiving weekend of 2002. Melinda and I joined them for dinner on Saturday night at their home in Columbus. The Davis house had been built in 1817 and was a "fixer-upper" when they moved into it in 1986. By 2002 three of their five kids had moved out on their own. Jackie, the mother, explained to me that they always felt that "our big, old house was a blessing from the Lord for us and we committed early on to allow Him to use it as a refuge for others as He saw fit."

Now it was my turn to be blessed by the Davises and their "big, old house." The Davises were not wealthy, except in the things that really mattered: faith, hope, and love. In those things they were positively rich, and I was about to be blessed by that wealth.

Melinda's brother Chuck had explained to Jackie and her husband Bill that, "A young man from Russia is coming to Columbus to attend Franklin University for two years to get his associate's degree in Business. He needs a place to stay." They agreed to host me for two years, beginning in December 2002 and I moved in just after Christmas.

The Davises gave me the largest of their spare bedrooms and I quickly found a home for my possessions. It would be nice to have a place to call my own for a while. I was told that I was not to consider myself a guest in the house, but to make myself at home, helping myself to anything I needed.

School got underway and I took my studies seriously. At twenty-five, I was older than many of the students, and I saw college as my job, what God had for me at that time. Jackie, a former English teacher, was a big help to me as I worked on all of my papers. I could speak English well—most people comment that they don't even notice an accent—but I had never had to commit those words to writing like I did at Franklin. To write a short email to a friend is one thing, but in college I was expected to write paper after paper, and they would be graded! Jackie did her best to teach me English grammar, my biggest shortcoming, along the way.

Two of the Davis kids were still living at home. Ben, nineteen at the time, was living in the house's basement apartment with his buddy Jay, who was going through a rough time in his life and needed a friend and a place to stay. The Davises' daughter Rebekah, twenty-one, was also living at home for a while, after finishing her own two-year associate's degree.

From my immigrant's perspective, I thought Ben and Bekah were selfish, lazy, and spoiled. I never said anything, but my lack of patience for post-high school American kids trying to figure out what to do with their lives was probably pretty obvious to the Davises. It didn't help that Ben and Bekah were always having friends over and constantly leaving a mound of dirty dishes in their wake. Jackie no doubt smiled to herself, realizing that her two youngest weren't the only ones under her roof who had some growing up to do when I moved in. I initially got along better with the three older kids, Natalie, Lara, and Sarah, who were not living at home. Today, I have a great deal of respect for both Ben and Bekah, and a wonderful relationship with all of the Davis clan.

I became a big fan of the United States Postal Service. Every day I would run down the driveway to get the mail as soon as the mailman delivered it. I would separate the piles for each household member and would inform them what was in their pile before they even got to it. It irritated me how indifferent they were to their mail! The worst was when I would see Jackie throw some into the trash without even opening it—I opened *everything* addressed to me, even "junk" mail. When they asked me, after several months, why I was obsessed with the mail, I explained that for eighteen years of my life I had never gotten a personal piece of mail. An envelope, addressed to me, regardless of content, was an affirmation that I mattered to someone. I was glad when Jackie told me that my appreciation for the little things in life—things like the mail, hot showers, having a washer and dryer, your own bathroom—have helped all of them to be more grateful.

Very early on I asked Bill and Jackie to please tell me if I ever said or did anything to hurt or offend them. I also asked them to communicate any expectations they had of me. With that, I settled into quiet observation for a time. It soon became clear to me that the Davises are a very close-knit family. Bill and Jackie are very connected with their kids and grandchildren.

Growing up, I often thought of the parents I never had, but I had given little thought to the *family* I never had. I loved becoming a part of the Davis family. In addition to their closeness, I was surprised how down-to-earth, relaxed, and free-flowing they were. Friends and family would come and go from the house all the time—not formal, scheduled events, just comings and goings. It was a fun, relaxing atmosphere unlike anything I had ever experienced.

It had been my experience, thus far, that in general, Russians had fewer friends than Americans, but those friendships were much deeper. In my mind, Americans tended to have friendships a mile long but an inch deep, whereas Russians tended to have friendships an inch long but a mile deep. Americans, I thought, were more open and inviting and polite, but the spark may go out just as quickly as it was lit, or the depth of the relationship never gets much beyond the politeness. Russians, on the other hand, tend to be much more reserved and skeptical and cold, but once they connect with each other, it would take something very major to sever that relationship. I will admit that those observations may be oversimplified, but they were very real perceptions to me, nonetheless. In a very short period of time, the Davis family dispelled those notions. Their relationships were both long and deep.

In addition to their younger kids, I also became friends with the older three Davis children. In fact, their daughter Sarah and her husband Nathan even adopted Russian twins. They named the boys Riley and Kaden. Much to my surprise, they gave Riley the middle name of Alexander, in my honor. The adoption process gave the whole family a firsthand experience with Russian orphanages and strengthened our growing bond even more deeply.

Twenty-two months old when they were adopted, the twins did not know how to chew and swallow solid food. There was no time in the orphanage for the workers to sit and feed the many hungry infants; the children were taught at a very young age to handle their own bottle. Once they learned to chew, they would chew and chew and chew a bite of food, but they had no grasp of understanding how to swallow it.

Poor little Riley was pretty sickly. His crossed eyes, coupled with his skinny frame and inability to eat, made his wheezing and coughing all the more pathetic. In that first year in America, he spent more than his fair share of time in ambulances and emergency rooms. After months of breathing treatments at home each night, he had surgery to remove his tonsils, along with several surgeries to correct his lazy eye. He is now doing great and looks quite distinguished in his glasses.

I have no doubt that little Riley would have ended up in the orphanage for sickly kids, confined his entire lifetime to a crib and would likely not be alive today to see his seventh year of life.

Helping Sarah and Nathan with their adoption was just the beginning of the Lord using me in that role in America. Throughout my time in the U.S. the Lord has repeatedly brought people my way who were in the process of trying to adopt from Russia, and, often, those who have already adopted, who desperately need assistance and encouragement. At just about every gathering of believers in which I find myself to tell my story, there is someone who knows a family that I "just have to meet."

The older the child is, when adopted, the more complex the problems and the greater the challenges. My life story illustrates that well, and it has been a real privilege for me to assist in whatever ways I can. But that has been a pastime to my larger purpose for The Harbor.

Three fortunate boys from Russia. Even though it's several years old, I love this picture. That's Riley on the left and Kaden on the right

24

*How great is your goodness, which you have stored
up for those who fear you, which you bestow in the
sight of men on those who take refuge in you.*
                                        —Psalm 31:19

While I may have been in my mid-twenties during
my college career, in many ways I was experiencing
childhood for the first time. I'm sure that's the way it came
across to the Davises as I would sometimes act just plain
goofy. At the mall with some of the grandkids I would take
off, running down the mall pushing the stroller, giggling
along with the grandkids at the speed at which the stores
streamed by us. When I wrestled with the grandsons, I
would have as much fun as they would. It wasn't just when
the grandchildren were around, either. I was known to be
a terror with grocery carts in the stores and parking lots,
often attracting stares from other customers.

The Davises never reprimanded me for my silly behavior. They always pointed it out, and often teased me about
it, but somehow they sensed that it was a necessary part of
my growing up. There was no way for someone to go back
and rock me to sleep, but rocking one of the grandbabies
to sleep seemed to help fill some of the gaps from my own
childhood. In many ways, the Davis grandkids, with their
childish, imaginative play, were instruments of healing
for me. Being around such a family made me all the more

passionate about helping folks adopt children from the orphanages in Russia.

There is a phenomenon with orphans, at least for those who grew up in an orphanage, that goes contrary to expectations: a sense of entitlement that comes from years of someone else providing for you. Never mind that their core needs of love and affection were never met, or that their provisions were secondhand, ill-fitted clothing and shoes, or that their showers were cold. Their perceived needs were always met by someone else—and not anyone close to them, either, but by an impersonal "them." Similarly, there is a concept with orphans known as "silent love": their inability to express appreciation. They were never taught how to show appreciation or express affection.

I could readily recognize this in others. In all my work with the orphanages, and for all that I provided to them, my reward was seldom any outward appreciation. Admittedly, this was sometimes discouraging, but I had to constantly remind myself why I was doing what I was doing. It takes a long time for orphans to show love and appreciation to anyone. Looking back on my own eighteen years in the orphanage system, Melana was the only person to whom I could show any love or appreciation. It was an eye-opening experience for me when I first noticed little kids in America saying "please" and "thank you" and showing appreciation and affection to adults, more foreign to me than the language.

I am sure that people were baffled at how picky I was when I first came to America (and still am, to some degree), but I attribute it to this sense of entitlement ingrained in orphans. For someone with few possessions and no income, my tastes were decidedly expensive. I would rather do without than settle for something less than the brand-name, expensive, labeled clothes and shoes.

At the same time, though, the Davises were also surprised to see how meticulous I was with my things. I frequently washed my tennis shoes. My Gap jeans hung, laundered and creased, in my closet like dress pants. I was more into quality than quantity, and I tended to that quality with diligence.

That diligence carried over to chores, as well. I found out later that one of the reasons why Ben and Bekah so seldom did their dishes when we were all living at the house was because they could never do them to my standards. I had an irritating habit where, if they rinsed a dish and put it in the dishwasher, I would re-rinse it and reload it "correctly."

My know-it-all attitude and pride continued to be thorns in my flesh, something I constantly need to bring before the Lord. I would like to think I have gotten better at them, and I probably have, but still there are times when loving friends have had to take me aside and do as Mark Cathey did, telling me I need to work on my humility.

Jackie Davis has an interesting perspective on my growth in this area. She says that my first real, extended experience of living with family has given me the opportunity, for the first time, to not have to prove anything to others. I didn't have to prove myself to her family. That unconditional love has given me the security we all need in order to live humble lives. I praise God for that, and continue to ask Him to continue to make me more like Him, rather than the selfish, "entitled," know-it-all orphan of my youth.

Ever since the possibility of an American education came my way when the Hugheses first offered it to me, it was my great goal. For seven years I had been waiting for another chance. When the Franklin University opportunity came up, I knew that it was going to be my last one. I had blown my chance before; I could not do it again.

Mark and Melinda Cathey tried to alleviate the pressure. They told me they did not expect me to get all A's and B's. They knew it would be hard for me, but they wanted me to enjoy the experience, too. Yet, I still put incredible pressure on myself. I would have preferred the four-year degree, but the timing wasn't right. The ministry could not afford the funds and they needed my full-time efforts as soon as possible.

Every day for two-and-a-half years (except for summers) I rode the bus to and from campus. I worked very hard and studied a lot. My classmates would often tease me that I studied too much and worked too hard. It was probably for that reason that I hated group projects—there were too many "slackers" who wouldn't contribute. Franklin is a commuter school so we didn't have the typical, traditional campus life. It was just as well: I was there for one purpose, to get my degree.

That day finally came in August 2005. I graduated from Franklin University, magna cum laude, with an associate's degree in Business Management. It was a very big day for me, a real milestone in my life. It was a long, long way from being a little boy in Russia, living on the streets of St. Petersburg.

The Davises put on a big celebration, and I mean big! Of course, the entire Davis clan was there. Melinda Cathey came in from Minnesota. Her husband Mark couldn't attend, but Melinda's brother Chuck came. That was significant since it was through Chuck that I got to live with the Davises. Rich and Sue Gregg came in all the way from California, and Punkin would not have missed it. I was nervous because, for the first time, the two women I called "Mom" would meet each other. Sue and Punkin are both

GRADUATION DAY
Top row: John Hughes, Bill Davis, and Rich Gregg; Middle row: Melinda Cathey, me, and Jackie Davis; Bottom row: Sue Gregg and Punkin Durio

wonderful, godly women and they bonded immediately; I need not have worried. Perhaps most significant to me, John Hughes, my original host on my first trip to America, accepted the Davises' invitation and was present for the celebration as well. His wife Thompson was sorry she was unable to attend, but I was thrilled to see John once again. It was a great opportunity for everyone to meet and get to know each other a little. It was both awkward and amazing for me to have them all in the same room at the same time.

The Davises gave me an "official" certificate of adoption into their family. It sealed the deal: no matter where the future took me, I would always and forever be considered as part of the Davis family. Rich Gregg gave a toast that day to mark the significance of the event and the moment in my journey. But the most moving part of all that day was the time of prayer we shared. I sat at the dining room table, everyone placed hands on me, and they all took turns praying for me.

For a graduation gift Punkin took me on a ten-day trip to Alaska. She had planned the entire trip and surprised me with it. She spared no expense or experience. We used every mode of transportation imaginable. In addition to the normal planes, trains, and automobiles, we also used a helicopter (to the top of a glacier!), a jeep, all-terrain vehicles, white water rafts, speed glacier boats, and a sea plane. We even went dog sledding (the highlight of my trip). I experienced more fun and adventure in one week than I had in my whole lifetime.

Now it was time to get to work, and I was excited to put my new degree, knowledge, and experience to work, doing the thing that I really loved: bringing God's love to the orphans of Russia.

The Davis clan celebrating an Ohio State football victory

25

Consequently, you are no longer foreigners and aliens, but fellow citizens with God's people and members of God's household.

—Ephesians 2:19

My mission was to raise the funds for The Harbor. In order for me to do that, however, I needed to maintain my legal status in the U.S. Even before I graduated I began the process of updating my visa. I was in the United States on a non-immigrant student visa that was good for three years, provided I was a student. Once I knew I would not be able to continue for a four-year degree I began to be concerned about my legal status. I was not prepared to be "shipped back" to Russia.

Patrick Schumer, who was the head of International Student Admissions at Franklin, had become a friend. He was a Christian and was excited about The Harbor and my life story. I went to him for help with my visa situation. He suggested I apply for Optional Professional Training (OPT), explaining to me that every foreign student who receives a degree can stay in the country for an additional year, pursuing their line of study. I applied and was accepted to practice my Business Management degree for one year in the United States. Ninety days before the OPT would expire, I would need to file for a new student visa or some other visa status, or I would have to leave the country.

Six months into my OPT, I filed for a religious worker visa and was approved for one year, with the possibility of an extension of two more years. In order to get that status, I needed Church Resource Ministries to vouch for my work on behalf of The Harbor. For my "religious worker" status to be legal I would also need to draw regular pay. CRM put me on a salary of $1,000 a month. The good news was that for the first time in my life I would have a steady paycheck. The bad news was that I now needed to raise enough funds to support both the ministry and the paycheck I was required to receive. The Harbor bank account was just about depleted by this time because I had not been able to fundraise for more than two years, so I had my work cut out for me.

While I was on my student visa, I was able to travel to and from the United States and I did so. The two summers I was in school I traveled back to Russia for a few months to help out with The Harbor in St. Pete. But once I received my OPT, and likewise the religious worker visa, if I left the U.S. I would not be able to return without applying for a whole new visa in Russia (and that was not likely to be approved).

The more I researched and the deeper I got into the world of visa applications and bureaucratic processes, the more I knew I needed help. John Hughes recommended an immigration attorney. Gloria was a real godsend. It took years but finally, in 2008, I was approved for a coveted United States "green card." That was the culmination of the prayers of many people in both of "my" countries.

I was thrilled when, after I got my green card, I was finally able to get my driver's license. Bill and Jackie taught me to drive and I passed the test. Now I not only had a college diploma, but an Ohio driver's license as well. I was worse than any sixteen-year-old, proudly showing off my driver's license to everyone I came in contact with. Bekah Davis sold me her 1999 Acura and I was able to pay her the entire amount with money I had saved up for the purpose.

A green card is good for ten years. As long as I pay the fee and renew it every decade, my legal status in the United States remains intact. I have all the rights of an American citizen, with the exception that I cannot vote, nor can I hold certain government positions. My ultimate goal is to be an American citizen. I would thus have dual citizenship, which seems fitting since I now spend nearly half my time in Russia and my purpose and passion are there, even while my life and love of country and any family I have ever known remain scattered throughout these United States.

26

But in your hearts set apart Christ as Lord. Always be prepared to give an answer to everyone who asks you to give the reason for the hope that you have. But do this with gentleness and respect.
—1 Peter 3:15

Because of my immigration status, I was not able to return to Russia for almost five years. In December 2008 I went back for four months. My old orphanage mates Sveta, Maria, and Ed met me at Melana's apartment for a wonderful reunion. Melana, who was now working as a nanny, said that her employer had an apartment for rent. It was some distance from the city, out on the Bay of Finland. It was only a small efficiency apartment, with a sofa that pulled out to a bed, but it was spotless and in a very nice area. I signed the lease. As with all Russian real estate, it was pricey. I would be paying $800 a month for rent, plus the cost of utilities.

Fortunately, during the process of upgrading my visa, I was required to also upgrade my salary to a minimum of $2,000 a month. I didn't have many needs, and I was more concerned with the needs of The Harbor, so I determined at that point that all of my expenses for the ministry would be taken from my salary, rather than other ministry funds. That would include all travel that I do for The Harbor throughout the U.S. and to and from Russia. It's a practice I continue to this day, and the Lord has honored it. I have never found myself lacking anything I need.

While I was willing to splurge on the luxury of my own efficiency apartment, I was very frugal when it came to food. In Russia I ate mostly bread, potatoes, and pasta; not necessarily the healthiest diet, but the least expensive.

When I saw our director, Luba, the first day, she said, "I'll give you one day to rest up and recuperate from your travels, but first thing the next morning, I need you to go to work."

While I was still in America and unable to get to Russia, the work of The Harbor continued. The Lord had worked lots of miracles and our vision for a vocational training center had gotten off the ground. Luba and her team had even gotten the government to approve it for orphans still in the orphanages to attend, in addition to the Harbor kids and street children. They offered an array of classes that changed each quarter, depending upon the availability of instructors. Part of my job while in Russia was to teach some courses at the training center. That particular summer I taught computer and English courses.

I also used my time to disciple and mentor orphans, including current and former residents of The Harbor and kids still living in the orphanages. It was a time for me to reconnect with friends, network with churches and government officials, and recruit new volunteers and staff. I was also charged with finding a bigger facility for our vocational training center. Any free time I had, I visited orphanages.

Orphanage Number 18 is for "academically and/or mentally challenged" orphans. Anywhere from fourteen to twenty-five kids from Number 18, ages fifteen to eighteen years old, come to The Harbor's vocational training center one day a week. The kids get to pick what classes they want to take and they love the opportunity. On my first day at the vocational center, one little guy, Sasha, opened up to me and shared his entire life story. Luba was amazed, as Sasha had been attending for weeks and had never opened up like that. I didn't want to limit my time with these kids to just the one day a week they were at the center, so I added Orphanage 18 to my list and visited as often as possible.

The first time I arrived there, the boys were so excited to see me. They took me to their rooms and carefully showed me all of their few, but very special, personal possessions. One of the boys wanted to demonstrate to me how well he cleaned the bathroom. After watching the full bathroom cleaning demonstration, I treated the boys to cake and cookies.

Some of the boys from Orphanage Number 3, to whom I taught English on that trip to Russia, have since graduated from the orphanage system. I continued to keep up with them via email and online video chats and I was able to continue mentoring and befriending them.

My visits to the orphanages gave me a chance to build relationships with the boys and also with the caregivers, which was helpful in building credibility for The Harbor.

Sometime before my trip, I had been contacted by David Ford, an American missionary in Kaluga, a city of about four hundred thousand just south of Moscow. David worked a lot with orphans and had learned about the work of The Harbor up in St. Petersburg. He was very interested in starting a similar work in Kaluga. When he heard that I was going to be back in Russia, he called The Harbor to see if I would be willing to come down and meet with him.

I made the eight-hour train trip to Kaluga and spoke at David's church about my life and the Harbor ministry. This was a small church of only about thirty people, meeting in a rented room above a store, but, despite its size and outward appearance, it was the most vibrant church I had ever seen in Russia. Pastor Dima's wife had died at the age of thirty-five, leaving him to raise their two young children himself. I was impressed with what a wonderful job he was doing with the church and with his children. David was the only foreigner in the church; the rest of the congregation were all Russian Christians.

After I spoke, one woman, whose kids were grown, stood up to say, "I want to be the first 'mother' in our Harbor that we start down here!"

I met a young man, Sergei, who was a former drug addict who had spent time in prison. It was in prison that he had found the Lord, and felt called by God, once he was released, to form a ministry and rehab center for drug addicts. To my amazement, that ministry was fully supported by this small body of believers.

The church asked me to stay and speak to a special meeting of their youth the next evening. There were about thirty young people, along with most of the adults who had heard me the day before. Of the thirty young people in attendance, about half of them were orphans who attended this church. I shared for a couple of hours and allowed time for questions and answers. The youth were attentive, almost captivated, and very engaged in the discussion time.

At the end of the their time, Sergei stood and said, "I need to pray for you." It was a sweet time of prayer, and Sergei prayed specifically that God would anoint me and the church so they could start a Harbor in their city.

After the service, a visitor, who, like the pastor, was named Dima, approached me and introduced himself. He said that he was a consultant for non-profits and would like to help with the local government officials in our effort to get the program going in Kaluga. In one of those great coincidences that only the Lord could orchestrate, he just happened to be visiting this tiny church that evening. He invited Pastor Dima and me to go the next day with him to meet with the Minister of Social Welfare for the entire Kaluga region.

We met the next morning at a beautiful government office building known as "the white house." The minister listened to my brief life story and as I described the work of The Harbor. He then looked at me and said, "So, what can I do for you?" I asked only for his support to start a program in Kaluga.

"I cannot help you because it is a Christian ministry and that is out of my jurisdiction," he said.

Just as I was prepared to thank him for his time and depart, he picked up the phone and set up an appointment for us to immediately meet with the Minister of Education and Science, the appropriate government official. To receive an appointment like that, and so quickly, is unheard of in Russia, a country well-known for its bureaucratic minefields.

Moments later, the two Dimas and I had an audience with Antoinina. She was very formal and all business. She begrudgingly listened to our talk of The Harbor. Suddenly, I felt like the Lord wanted me to talk a little about my life and my background, so I gave the thirty-second version.

Her demeanor instantly changed.

"Tell me more," she said.

After I obliged, she asked the same question that the

government official in St. Petersburg had asked: "What about all the other orphans?" In the next moments I felt like I was given words that were not my own. I gave an impassioned response about how we could not help all the orphans, but that I had seen the value of helping one orphan at a time, setting them up as role models. I talked about the number of Harbor graduates who were already ministering to orphans in the orphanages and many who had come back to volunteer at The Harbor. Frankly, I was surprised at the picture I was able to paint and the passion with which I was able to convey our vision; it could only have come from the Lord.

Antoinina immediately stood up and shook my hand. She said, "I support your mission." She then pointed to Pastor Dima and said, "Who are you?"

She was unimpressed that he was a pastor when she learned that his church was not Orthodox. She was, however, quite impressed with his answer to her next question, "Who will run this ministry?" The pastor unhesitatingly replied, "My church."

At that point, Antoinina softened and opened up to us as friends. She told us that she had started her own nonprofit in 2003 to help emancipated orphans. "I have never, until now, met anyone else who shares my passion." Even more astounding, she then stated, "I'd like to give you my non-profit; turn over my organization to you to run."

What took The Harbor three years to accomplish in St. Petersburg took thirty minutes in Kaluga. I thought back to Sergei's prayer at the service the night before. God had certainly delivered what he asked for and anointed our efforts that morning.

At this writing, the work in Kaluga has a long way to go, but the experience of that morning gave me a good occasion to reflect. A mere decade before, I was a "nobody," a number, and one of hundreds of thousands of nobodies who were a blight on Russian society. I had no family, no direction, no purpose, and no hope. Now here I was, in the offices of two rather lofty, regional government officials, sharing my story, touching their hearts, and, rather ironically, providing them with the solution to their "blight." Even better than that, though, I had a purpose, direction, hope, and "family" who loved me unconditionally, all thanks to a loving God who reached out and found me. For my part, all I contributed was a willingness to serve Him in faith. Ephesians 3:20 was certainly true in my life: "Now all glory to God, who is able, through his mighty power at work within us, to accomplish infinitely more than we might ask or think."

27

*Never be lacking in zeal, but keep your spiritual
fervor, serving the Lord.*

—Romans 12:11

Back stateside, I continued to fundraise for The Harbor and also help couples with their adoption efforts. I'll use a couple in Columbus as an example of an adoptive family that I have been honored to help.

During the many months the difficult legal process takes, I continued to encourage this couple on, even when they were tempted to give up. Sometimes it helps just to have someone around who has "been there." When they finally took physical custody of the eight-year-old, they had to remain in Russia for a week. I was in Columbus, but we managed to speak frequently during that time. The combination of the language barrier (the child spoke no English and they spoke little Russian) and other complications made that week extremely difficult. By the time I greeted them at the Columbus airport things had only gotten worse. One parent was extremely overwhelmed with the relentless stresses added. I should add that this is not uncommon in adoption situations, particularly when the child is not an infant.

Over the next few months I spent lots of time with the family and occasionally I would take their child for a time and let him stay with us at the Davises for an evening or overnight to give the parents a break.

Those first six months were difficult. It was not only the language barrier and behavior issues that came from the child's "baggage," but the adjustments of this childless couple, now suddenly parents, and not of a newborn, but an eight-year-old with his own struggles to adjust to a whole new life. Again, this is not uncommon, but that doesn't lessen the hardship. It is my privilege to walk alongside folks like these as they seek to obey God's will for their lives and help "one of the least of these." The transformation of their son and that family, has been nothing short of miraculous. In between my Harbor fundraising engagements I make it a priority to counsel with many adoptive parents and their former Russian orphans as they struggle through the transition.

Though I enjoy helping adoptive families, my full-time work is The Harbor and I spend the majority of my time traveling throughout the United States sharing our story. I still call Columbus home, but I am usually only there for a few days at a time between my trips. Armed with my green card, I travel to Russia at least once a year, usually in the summer, to work at The Harbor.

I have been to a lot of churches in the United States and in Russia. I love the big mega-churches, just because it is impressive to see so many believers together at one time. The preaching is generally great. Maybe if I was more stationary and not traveling so much, I could learn to call one of these big churches home by becoming involved in a small group and finding some community. But that would be really hard for me with all my travels. I love the warmth and love and community I have found in Meadowbrook and in Village Vineyard, two small churches in the Columbus area that I attend. And, like the little church in Kaluga, I am amazed (and really touched) by the generosity and outreach of these little churches. They tend to be much more outward thinking (of others and their needs) than focused on their own needs.

When The Harbor started, our staff consisted of Luba, the director, Katya, the psychologist, Ira, the mentor, and Pavel, the pastor. There were no Russian churches involved, but the Lord did enable us to establish a partnership of sorts with one of the largest Christian universities in the country, St. Petersburg Christian University. From there we have gotten staff from their graduate students, with degrees in theology, counseling, pedagogy, and teaching. Early on, there were a few churches in the States supporting our work, but it was primarily individuals who significantly stepped in to partner with the ministry.

The first group of residents were the four girls, two of whom were brought from a street shelter by a police officer after taking them off the streets (they had been sold into prostitution by their parents when they were just eight and nine years old). Of the other two girls, one came from my former orphanage, Number 51, and the other came from the Voice of the Children shelter that The Harbor was partnered with back then.

Those first four girls were a real challenge for our young ministry, which had plenty of vision but very little experience. At times it was just plain hard to deal with the girls and their "baggage." The Lord tested the faith of all of us workers, but He also reminded us that we shouldn't give up on the girls because He never gives up on any of us. Thus, we committed ourselves to disciple them just as Christ would.

A year into the ministry, one of the initial residents left The Harbor to go back to prostitution because it was all she knew and, to her, it was the easy way out. We knew the Lord wanted more for her, and we tried to lovingly communicate to her the dangerous consequences of her decision. Because the word "consequence" is practically non-existent in an orphan's vocabulary, our admonitions did not make any difference. We prayed for her and communicated that the doors of The Harbor family were always open to her, but she left and never chose to come back. The other three girls completed the two-year residential program with The Harbor. One of them stayed on for two more years.

In the third year of our ministry The Harbor was approved by the Russian Committee of Education and Science and the Committee of Justice as a "St. Petersburg Charitable Public Organization that transitions orphans after orphanage emancipation." With that official approval, The Harbor now had a green light to go directly into the orphanages and select residents into the program.

After four years of ministry, we opened another apartment and had boys in our program as well. We were now ministering to young adult men and women, ages sixteen through twenty-three, graduating them every two years and replacing each with another young adult. The Lord began to change and transform the lives of The Harbor graduates. More and more of the residents were receiving their education, accepting Jesus as their personal Savior, and changing inside and out.

After five years, The Harbor purchased its first facility, the girls' apartment, and rented more apartments. The original goal was to purchase four apartments to accommodate forty residents at any one time in the ministry. But five years into our work and we were not there yet. It was not easy, and we frequently prayed and asked God why He had not allowed us to grow as we had envisioned.

Little did we know we were simply not ready and the time was not yet right. The Harbor had to establish the foundation before the growth could happen.

Melinda Cathey and I were encouraged by the opportunity to speak at a club of businesswomen in St. Pete. I will never forget the experience. We went to that building and noticed more Mercedes-Benzes, BMWs, and Audis than either of us had ever seen. The women were nicely dressed and quite occupied with drinking expensive champagne and eating black caviar. After this extravagant time they asked us to share about The Harbor.

As we were talking, we noticed that many of the women were basically uninterested. Some were even falling asleep! I was ready to apologize for bothering them. As soon as we were done they simply went on with their program, having a good time and spending astounding amounts of money, but on earthly things. It was a good indication to us that the chances of raising funds in Russia, even among the wealthy, were practically nonexistent, at least for now.

We also began approaching American corporations for gifts, but after much effort we realized that, too, was a dead-end.

Meanwhile, by year five the Lord was bringing more and more individuals to partner with our ministry. Over the years God had brought so many people into my life—from the very poor to the very wealthy. I saw an amazing contrast in that. I had spoken to churches as small as six people and as large as seven thousand. What I learned is that God's economy and math do not match the world's. You would think that the larger the church, the more we would receive from them. Such has not been the case. He has continually richly blessed our ministry from those gatherings of a few people, yet almost nothing from the groups with big numbers of members. I continue to be grateful for all of our supporters, both those who are able to give large sums of money and those who can only donate small amounts. God understands the heart and He delights to use the "widow's mite" as well as the larger gifts we receive.

Today, The Harbor has the support of hundreds of individuals who are our faithful and committed ministry partners. We also receive funding from over a dozen churches, representing seven different denominations, and some charitable trusts and foundations.

On average, we have twenty orphans in the residential program at any given time, and minister to more than one hundred twenty orphans in the vocational training center. There are five different local St. Petersburg churches that are now praying for the ministry and one church has recently adopted The Harbor as their main mission to support. The Russian government is actively participating with us, especially in our vocational training center, because they see the potential and power of transformation.

Furthermore, our staff have trained different ministries from six cities in Russia to replicate the model of The Harbor in their communities. We are now even advising other ministries in other countries how to replicate what we have done, especially in the Commonwealth of Independent States (the former Soviet Republics). God is good!

28

*"For I know the plans that I have for you," declares
the Lord, "plans to prosper you and not to harm
you, plans to give you a hope and a future."*
—Jeremiah 29:11

It would seem that I have made up for the lost years of
my life that lacked loving relationships, guidance, and
affection. While I was never officially adopted, both Sue
and Punkin have filled motherly roles in my life, and the
Davises and Catheys have become family. In Russia, Misha
and Marina have been my aunt and uncle, and Melana will
always hold a very precious part of my heart.

I have received wise counsel and life instruction from
godly men in my life: Mark Cathey, John Hughes, Rich
Gregg, Mel Duke, and Bill Davis, among others.

A few years ago I got a distressing phone call from Mary
Lou Duke. Rounding out my family, she and Mel had been
like grandparents to me. She was calling to tell me Mel
had an aneurism that burst. He was on life support and
not expected to live.

Upset, I did not know what to do. I was scheduled to
leave early the next morning for ministry engagements
in Texas. The flights were booked and paid for, and there
were people expecting me. I was torn. I knew there was
nothing I could do for Mel, but I felt compelled to go to
Colorado to say goodbye to this sweet and good man who

had been like a grandfather to me, even if he was not aware that I was there.

I instinctively called Punkin, one of my "moms," to ask her advice. She concurred with what the Davises had been telling me: "Alex, you *need* to be there."

I paid the fee to change my flight to Colorado and called Mary Lou to tell her I was on my way. At 2:00 AM a phone call from Mary Lou jarred me from my restless sleep. Mel had died. I wept for about forty-five minutes, literally crying myself to sleep.

The next morning I called Punkin to tell her, and her response was, "Why didn't you call me?"

"At two in the morning?" I asked, perplexed.

"Alex, I meant it when I said that I am here for you *anytime* you need me."

After that incident I was better able to gauge my relationships. Aside from the mile long/mile deep description, I came to understand that those few people who meant the most to me were people that I would drop anything for if they needed me. If anyone in my Davis family, or if Sue or Punkin or Melana or Melinda needed me for anything, I would drop what I am doing and be there.

I had never experienced the death of one so dear to me as Mel. It was both extremely painful and incredibly encouraging to feel that loss and pain. I flew to Colorado and was warmly welcomed by Mary Lou and her family to share in their grief, just as if I was one of their own.

I have lived in many homes for short and extended stays. For someone with no "real" family of my own, the Lord has blessed me with many, many folks who have shared their love with me. Maybe this orphan does have a family after all.

When I think back on this journey, I am touched at how

God used so many different people to impact my life. The one thing they have in common—from the first missionaries I met after the fall of the Soviet Union, on through to the people who partner with The Harbor today—is a desire to be obedient to God's call on their lives and to share His love in a practical way. How different my life would have been if it had not been for some crazy Americans who went out of their way to come to Russia for short-term missions projects and made their way to Orphanage Number 51. Or if Melana had not taken us under her protective wing. Or if Melinda and Mark had not opened their door to an unknown, t-shirted young man shivering in the cold St. Petersburg night. Praise God they did, and that now, I have the opportunity to do the same thing for others.

ജ

"Though my father and mother forsake me,
the Lord will receive me."
PSALM 27:10

A NOTE ON THE WRITING OF THIS BOOK

While my family may have had some experiences in sharing our home over the years, we were not prepared for the impact that Alex Krutov would have on our lives. We were not prepared for the bond we formed that will last a lifetime; the "adoption," as it were, of this young man at the age of twenty-five into our family. We could not adopt him if we wanted to—he's thirty-three now—yet in all respects he is family. More than eight years later, and he is still living with us.

Of course, we learned his story early on in our relationship, his background, and what brought him to America, but the more we've gotten to know him, the more remarkable that story becomes. I've vowed for years to write his story for him. I have no doubt that it can be a blessing to others. I also have no doubt that this compelling urge to share it is a prompting from the Lord.

The purpose of this book is for you to meet Alex. This is his story, and more profoundly for all of us, it is really God's story. We all, including Alex, are just the vessels. More important than Alex's survival in the Russian orphanage system, and even more important than his ministry today, his life story is a story of hope; the story of God's protection and calling on his life. While Alex's heart and ministry is clearly for orphans, his life story speaks to the power of God for anyone living without hope.

He and I have worked on this book for three years now. When the thought came to me originally in early 2008 to get his story on paper, we worked together feverishly for a time. It is a long, slow process. We sit for hours and talk;

me prodding him with questions and him telling story upon story while I frantically try to listen and write at the same time. I filled several legal pads with notes before hitting the computer and trying to put some semblance of chronology and meaning to the various memories and stories. Being as busy as I am with full-time work and thirteen grandkids, as I got farther and farther behind in transcribing the stories to print, I became more and more reluctant to hear more stories and take more notes.

About the time I began to get caught up, Alex's travels picked up. For the first time in five years he was able to go back to Russia. While thrilled for him, the book came to a screeching halt when he was gone for almost three months at a time twice in 2009.

Alex is still young and in many ways his ministry and his life are just beginning. I can't even imagine what else the Lord has in mind for him. This much I know for certain: God has a calling on this young man's life. God has given him a new heart and put a new spirit into him. He has removed his heart of stone and given him a heart of flesh (Ezekiel 36:26); He has lifted Alex "out of the slimy pit, out of the mud and mire" and set his feet upon a rock and given him a firm place to stand (Psalm 40:1–2). I marvel at the work God has done in and through Alex's life and I count it a privilege to have been a part these eight-plus years.

I felt compelled by the Lord to write this book, but I don't know how He is going to use it. Maybe it will inspire just one couple to adopt just one little child still trapped behind the walls of a Russian orphanage, longing to be held and loved. If it gives even one child a hope and a future, it has been worth the effort. If it is used to encourage those who have adopted to stick with the difficult transition process, or if it encourages even one troubled teenager to find hope again, it has been worth the effort. If it prompts anyone to support the work of The Harbor (www.theharborspb.org), which will in turn affect the lives of those graduate orphans, praise God! If Alex's life story beckons anyone to the cross and the saving grace of Jesus, Alex and I are both in awe that the Lord would see fit to use us in that process. Find a Bible-believing church near you and grow in that love and grace. And be prepared to "pay it forward" one day when the Lord calls upon you to be used in the life of another. Probably when you least expect it, maybe when you feel least prepared for it, that opportunity will come upon you and catch you totally off guard. Welcome that opportunity!

Isaiah 49 says, "Can a mother forget the baby at her breast and have no compassion on the child she has borne? Though she may forget, I will not forget you! See, I have engraved you on the palms of my hands." I can't imagine a mother forgetting her baby; having no compassion on her child. Yet, neither can I know Alex's mother's heart or judge her actions. I know only that I am thankful for this young man's life and blessed that the Lord saw fit to bring him into our lives.

The Harbor is now in its tenth year. The Lord has allowed this little ministry to raise over two million dollars, primarily through the efforts and faith of one Russian orphan, who survived his eighteen years in the Russian orphanage system, and was called by God, and responded to that call, to make a difference in the lives of other orphans. To God be the glory!

—JACKIE DAVIS
FEBRUARY 2011

The Harbor

Anchoring Lives. Launching Hope. Restoring Nations.

To learn more about
how you can support the
ministry of The Harbor,
please visit
theharborspb.org

Other exciting stories of faith

You might enjoy these other titles from Whitecaps Media

The Diaries of Jim Rayburn
edited by Kit Sublett
ISBN 978-0-9758577-7-9

Jim Rayburn was the founder of Young Life and one of the great men of faith of the 20th century. His journals recount his struggles and triumphs, making a fascinating read.

Coaching Third:
The Keith LeClair Story
by Bethany Bradsher
ISBN 978-0-9826353-0-8

LeClair achieved great success as a college baseball coach until the diagnosis of ALS forced him to change his priorities. Truly inspiring.

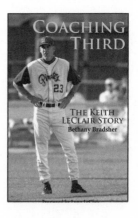

Find out how to order these books at
whitecapsmedia.com

Colophon

Infinitely More by Alex Krutov as told to Jackie Davis

Book created using Adobe InDesign CS3 and designed and edited by Kit Sublett for Whitecaps Media. Original manuscript prepared in Microsoft Word

Main body composed in Calluna and Calluna Sans, both designed by Jos Buivenga. Chapter numbers and some headings are composed in Kremlin Duma. Drop caps at the start of each chapter are set in Kremlin Samovar. Both Kremlin fonts are by Bolt Cutter Design. The title on the cover is set in Mistral

Cover image of the Church of the Resurrection of Christ in St. Petersburg by Anton Sokolov, istockphoto.com

Interior photos are from the private collections of the authors

Infinitely More was written and produced from start to finish on Apple Macintosh computers